# *The* Creed
## *a* CATECHIST'S GUIDE

### UNDERSTANDING
### AND SHARING
### WHAT WE BELIEVE

Janet Schaeffler, OP

**TWENTY-THIRD PUBLICATIONS**
A Division of Bayard
One Montauk Avenue, Suite 200
New London, CT 06320
(860) 437-3012 or (800) 321-0411
www.23rdpublications.com

ISBN 978-1-62785-035-3
Library of Congress Control Number: 2014946269

Printed in the U.S.A.

# Contents

# CHAPTER ONE

# The Creeds: What? When? How?

Have you ever asked (or been asked) "What do Catholics believe?" and struggled to know where to begin? In reality, we shouldn't find it an effort, because the creeds tell it all. Well, perhaps not all, because we do have such a rich expression of our tradition through Scripture, Tradition, liturgy, prayer, dogmas, doctrines, theologies, sacraments and symbols, values, ethics and laws, spiritualities, models of holy people, songs, music, dance, drama, art, architecture, festivals and feasts, and holy places. But our creeds do summarize for us the essence, the core, of our belief.

The simple declarative sentence "Jesus is Lord" is a miniature creed, that is, a statement or profession of belief. The church has promulgated some official creeds, most notably the Apostles' Creed and the Nicene Creed, both of which expressed the faith of the early Christian communities. *Their* faith remains *our* faith today.

The word *creed* comes from the Latin *credo*, which means "I believe." What Christians really proclaim is, "We believe." We do not invent our own faith; we receive it from God

1

through the church. As the Hippocratic Oath binds doctors into a community of healers, so our praying of our creeds unites us to our sisters and brothers in the faith.

It is important to keep in mind that the translation into "I/we believe" is active, which denotes not just a body of beliefs but a profession of faith. This faith is trust; not "I believe that" (although that certainly is included), but "I believe in."

## The Apostles' Creed

An ancient tradition holds that on the day of Pentecost, the apostles composed this creed under the guidance of the Holy Spirit, each apostle writing one of the twelve articles of the Creed. Historical research leads scholars to now believe that this is not the case, but the Apostles' Creed has always been considered to be a true summary of the beliefs of the apostles themselves.

Its origin (around 215 AD) was the profession of faith used in the instruction of catechumens and in the liturgy of baptism. The person to be baptized responded to three questions, divided according to the Persons of the Trinity.

The clearly Trinitarian structure of the profession of faith and the Apostles' Creed was likely intended to counter some early teachings (for example, by Marcion) that denied that the God of the Old Testament was the same God revealed in Jesus. This Trinitarian formulation would remain the basic structure of all the early creeds.

The Apostles' Creed is used by Roman Catholics, Anglicans, and many Protestant churches. Orthodox Christians do not disagree with any statement in the Apostles' Creed, but they do not use it because it does not have the authority of an ecumenical council.

The *Catechism of the Catholic Church* follows the Apostles' Creed in its presentation of the faith (with constant reference to the Nicene Creed, which is often more explicit and more detailed).

### The Apostles' Creed

I believe in God, the Father almighty,
Creator of heaven and earth,
and in Jesus Christ, his only Son, our Lord,
who was conceived by the Holy Spirit,
born of the Virgin Mary,
suffered under Pontius Pilate,
was crucified, died, and was buried;
he descended into hell;
on the third day he rose again from the dead;
he ascended into heaven,
and is seated at the right hand of God the Father almighty;
from there he will come to judge the living
    and the dead.
I believe in the Holy Spirit,
the holy catholic Church,
the communion of saints,
the forgiveness of sins,
the resurrection of the body,
and life everlasting. Amen.

This book will explore and reflect upon these lines, these prayerful beliefs, of the Apostles' Creed as we look at some of Catholicism's core beliefs.

## The Nicene Creed

For centuries, Catholics have been professing their faith in the Triune God during liturgy by proclaiming the Nicene Creed. This Creed clearly formulates essential Christian doctrines about God the Father, Son, and Holy Spirit, the church, salvation, and human destiny.

The Nicene Creed was crucial in Catholic history. Because of decades of controversy begun by a learned Egyptian priest, Arius, who denied that Jesus, the Son, always existed with the Father, the Nicene Creed came to birth. In effect, Arius denied Jesus' divinity and, therefore, the church's developing understanding of the doctrine of the Trinity.

This raging Arian controversy caused extreme dissension in the church. As a result, the Emperor Constantine convoked the first ecumenical council at Nicaea in 325. (Nearly all those who attended came from the eastern Mediterranean region.)

A major achievement of this council was to declare clearly the divinity of Jesus by issuing the Nicene Creed. The second ecumenical council, Constantinople (381), endorsed and expanded it; the councils of Ephesus (431) and Chalcedon (451) later reaffirmed it.

The Nicene Creed is used by Roman Catholics, Anglicans, many Protestants, and the Eastern Orthodox (although the Eastern Orthodox reject the "and the Son" clause added in 589 AD affirming that the Spirit proceeds from the Father and the Son).

## *The Nicene Creed*

I believe in one God,
the Father almighty,
maker of heaven and earth,
of all things visible and invisible.
I believe in one Lord Jesus Christ,
the Only Begotten Son of God,
born of the Father before all ages.

God from God, Light from Light,
true God from true God,
begotten, not made, consubstantial with the Father;
through him all things were made.

For us men and for our salvation
he came down from heaven,
and by the Holy Spirit was incarnate of the Virgin Mary,
and became man.

For our sake he was crucified under Pontius Pilate,
he suffered death and was buried,
and rose again on the third day
in accordance with the Scriptures.

He ascended into heaven
and is seated at the right hand of the Father.
He will come again in glory
to judge the living and the dead
and his kingdom will have no end.

I believe in the Holy Spirit, the Lord, the giver of life,
who proceeds from the Father and the Son,
who with the Father and the Son is adored and glorified,
who has spoken through the prophets.

I believe in one, holy, catholic and apostolic Church.

I confess one Baptism for the forgiveness of sins
and I look forward to the resurrection of the dead
and the life of the world to come. Amen.

## *To Continue your Journey of Exploration*

### The Scriptural Basis of the Creeds

Creeds, in the developed sense, do not occur in Scripture. Yet, creeds express essential biblical truths. At the same time, Scripture itself offers some rudimentary creedal forms that provide models for later statements.

The "Shema" of the Old Testament (Deuteronomy 6:4–9) falls in this category, and many scholars regard Deuteronomy 26:5–9 as a little creed.

In the New Testament, many references to "traditions" (2 Thessalonians 2:15), the "word of the Lord" (1 Thessalonians 1:8), and the "preaching" (Romans 16:25) suggest that a common message formed a focus for faith from the beginning, while confession of Jesus as Christ (John 1:41), Son of God (Acts 9:20), Lord (Romans 10:9), and God (John 20:28; Romans 9:5; Titus 2:13) illustrates an obvious starting point for the development of creeds in public profession.

## The Functions of Creeds

Creeds are certainly first and foremost prayers to pray, yet they serve many purposes in our faith journey.

### Baptismal

The first creeds were probably in the context of baptism. A creed offered the candidates the opportunity to make the profession called for in Romans 10:8–10. At first the form of words would vary, but familiar patterns soon began to develop using a Trinitarian question and answer format.

### Instructional

Because of the baptismal profession of faith, creeds soon came to serve as the syllabus for catechetical instruction in Christian doctrine. All candidates were expected to acquire and display some understanding of the profession of faith they would make. A sincere commitment was coupled with intellectual apprehension.

### Doctrinal

The rise of heresies helped to expand the first creeds into the more developed formulas. A phrase like "maker of heaven and earth" was probably inserted to counteract the Gnostic separation of the true God from the Creator, while the reference to the virgin birth and the stress on Christ's death safeguarded the reality of Jesus' human life and ministry. The response to the Arian heresy produced other additions (notably "of one substance with the Father") designed to express Christ's essential deity. These modifications gave the creeds a new function as key to the proper understanding of Scripture and as tests of orthodoxy for the clergy.

## Liturgical

Because of their use in the baptism rituals in the early church, creeds have always had a liturgical function. Throughout the early church's history, most times of common prayer included some profession of faith. This led to the inclusion of the Nicene Creed into the Eucharist, first in the East, then in Spain, and finally in Rome. Placing the creed after the proclamation of Scripture made it possible for believers to respond to the gospel with an affirmation of faith.

## What is an Ecumenical Council?

The history of the Nicene Creed comes from the church's early ecumenical councils. The Catholic Church's most recent council was the Second Vatican Council, with four sessions from October 11, 1962, through December 8, 1965.

Just what is an ecumenical council?

An ecumenical council is the gathering of all the bishops of the world as opposed to regional or local gatherings. According to current church law, only the pope calls this type of council, and he alone sets its agenda. Acts of the council are binding when approved by the pope and the body of bishops and officially proclaimed by papal authority.

Roman Catholics consider there to have been twenty-one such councils. However, the only councils accepted as truly ecumenical by both the church of the East and the West are the first seven. The first four councils (Nicaea, Constantinople I, Ephesus, and Chalcedon) are recognized as normative for all churches that confess the Nicene and Apostles' Creeds, and the decrees of those four councils form the basis for ecumenical dialogues.

Councils have usually been called to confront heresies or

to foster needed reform in the church. Vatican II was the only council in the church's history that did not issue any condemnations of heresies or errors. It was the only council that addressed some of its documents to those outside the church ("persons of good will"), and it was the only council that directly spoke to the issue of ecumenism, reconciliation, and dialogue not only among Christians but among all the world's religious traditions.

## The Creeds: A Time to Reflect and Pray

Our creeds, whether the Nicene Creed, the Apostles' Creed, or an adaptation we write while studying and praying the Creed through this book, have to be a living statement of belief. By its very nature, a creed needs to connect our head and our heart. There is a difference between knowing the Creed and living it.

We are called to transform the ideas and knowledge of the Creed into our personal values, into the way we live our lives. The Apostles' Creed—as well as the Nicene Creed—has been and continues to be a treasures for the church.

Continued repetition of the Nicene Creed at Mass may gradually lull us into a false sense of understanding. When we allow ourselves time to reflect and pray, however, the Creed can always be ever new and challenging.

FOR YOUR REFLECTION AND CONVERSATION

- *At liturgy next week, think about the words you pray in the Creed. Are there any that you wonder about? Are there any that are comforting? Are there any that are challenging?*

*Discuss your thoughts with your family or a friend.*

- *If a non-Christian (or a visitor from another galaxy) would describe what a Christian believes from watching you, what would they say?*

- *Is there a difference, for you, in praying the Creed by yourself and praying it with a community?*

- *Do our creeds say anything about your family today, your parish life, our church, the challenges in our world?*

- *Which person of the Trinity is easiest for you to pray to: Father (Creator), Son (Redeemer), or Holy Spirit (Sustainer)? Why?*

## As You Deepen your Prayer

- *Imagine that you have never read, heard, or prayed a creed. What do you believe? Write your own creed.*

- *Using the Apostles' Creed or the Nicene Creed, write a short commentary or rewording of each sentence.*

- *Pray the Creed. After each sentence, pray a prayer of praise. A few days later, pray the Creed, praying a prayer of thanks after each sentence. Several days later, as you pray the Creed, pray a prayer of petition after each sentence.*

- *As you pray the Creed, reflect on which Scripture passages come to mind for the various sentences?*

# CHAPTER TWO

# *"I believe in God, the Father almighty, Creator of heaven and earth..."*

A little boy in a third-grade faith formation session was intently drawing a picture. Peering over his shoulder, the catechist asked him what he was doing. The small boy replied that he was drawing a picture of God. Gently the catechist told him that no one knows what God looks like. Innocently and confidently the budding artist replied, "They will when I'm done."

The mystery of God! We use words, symbols, definitions, pictures, and dogmas. Yet, ultimately, God is a mystery. The theologian Karl Rahner reminds us, "If you are talking about God and you think you know what you are talking about, you're a heretic." Rudolph Otto, in his classic *The Idea of the Holy*, said: "If the human mind could fully explain God, then God would cease to exist."

What do we profess about God the Father when we profess the Creed?

### We believe in one God, the Father...

Jesus called God the Father "Abba," a loving parent image to stress the intimacy of God with humanity. When we call God "Father," we are using the language of faith. This does not mean, however, that we cannot also describe God with feminine images.

In Scripture, God is sometimes referred to in feminine images, such as mother. In Isaiah 66:13, God says, "As a mother comforts her child, so will I comfort you." The *Catechism of the Catholic Church* (no. 239) reminds us that "God transcends the distinction between the sexes. (God) is neither man nor woman. (God) is God."

In Mark's gospel, the first recorded gospel, Jesus uses "father" as a reference to God four times. In John's gospel, the last of the gospels to be written, God is referred to as father 101 times. It seems that the farther away the church got from Jesus, the more patriarchal the language became—not because Jesus was patriarchal but because that was simply the reality of the times. Of course, God is Father, but God is also much more than that—more than we have words for. God is God.

### Almighty...

The word "almighty" occurs fifty-six times in Scripture. This word is used only for God. The literal meaning of the word translated "almighty" in the New Testament is "the One who has his hand on everything."

### Maker of heaven and earth...

St. Thomas Aquinas said, "God has given us two books of revelation. One is nature. The other is Scripture. We need to learn to read them both to understand the greatness of God." The *Catechism of the Catholic Church* (no. 2500) tells us that "even before revealing himself to man in words of truth, God reveals himself to [man] through the universal language of creation."

Many of us have learned about God from homilies, catechisms, religious education, and Scripture classes. Do we take as much time to read the "book of creation" to see what it tells us about our marvelous God? (The poet Gerard Manley Hopkins reminded us: "The world is charged with the grandeur of God.")

Reflect for a moment on the marvels of creation. Scientists tell us that the universe has a just-right gravitational force. If it were larger, the stars would be too hot and burn up too quickly and too unevenly to support life. If it were smaller, the stars would remain so cool, nuclear fusion would never ignite, and there would be no heat and light. The universe has a just-right average distance between stars. If it were larger, the heavy element density would be too thin for rocky planets to form, and there would only be gaseous planets. If it were smaller, planetary orbits would become destabilized. How could we think that all this happened by accident? Not a chance! There is a God, the maker of heaven and earth.

This section of the Creed also asks us: have we taken seriously our partnership with God as co-creators of this universe? At one point in our history, humans believed that all creation was theirs to have dominion over. In 1980, the U.S. bishops of the heartland published a statement, *Strangers and Guests*, which called us to stewardship, based on chapter 25 of the Book of Leviticus. Today, many theologians are challenging us to look at the model of companionship evidenced in Genesis 2.

Stewardship can imply that God began creation and then handed over its care to humanity, so much so that humans move to center stage in the drama of creation. Companionship keeps the relationship of God and humanity in balance. Companionship also recognizes the inherent goodness in all creation, rather than the belief that some parts of creation are objects to be used by other creatures. Companionship also challenges us to realize that more than the good of the individual is at stake. The common good, rather than individualism, is the focal point of our actions and decisions.

Perhaps the most important reality about our belief in, and relationship with, God is summarized in this story. A singing contest was held at a small parish church. One of the best trained operatic singers entered the competition. He sang a rendition of the Our Father which was flawless. No one else wanted to compete against him, but finally a nervous older gentleman of the parish was persuaded to try. As he began to sing, few could hear him. He faltered. Then slowly he found the strength to pour himself into it. His performance was far from technically perfect, but every heart was touched. When the judges awarded the old man the prize, the operatic singer contested, "Why him? Why not me? Wasn't I brilliant?"

They answered: "You knew the song. He knew the Father."

# *To Continue your Journey of Exploration*

## Images of God
In our quest to understand God throughout the ages, humanity has used various images and names for God. No one image tells the whole story; each one gives a little glimpse.

### *Images of God within Scripture*
As we read and pray with Scripture, we become more and more aware how many images, names, and titles are given to God. Each captures only one facet of how we—in our limited understanding—have experienced God. The varying images of God found within the Old and New Testaments can probably be grouped into various realities about human life:

- Images of God taken from personal relationships, for instance: father, mother, husband, female beloved, companion, bridegroom, friend, suffering servant, protector

- Images of God from political life, such as: advocate, liberator, king, warrior, judge

- Images of God from a wide array of human crafts and professions: good shepherd, dairymaid, farmer, laundress, construction worker, potter, sower of good seed, fisherman, midwife, merchant, physician, bakerwoman, teacher, writer, artist, nurse, metalworker, homemaker, woman giving birth, woman nursing her young, mother dedicated to child care

- Images of God derived from the animal kingdom, such

as: roaring lion, hovering mother bird, angry mother bear, protective mother hen

- Images of God from cosmic reality: light, cloud, rock, fire, wind, living water, refreshing water, life itself

### Images of God from Various Traditions

Every religious tradition has unique ways of imaging/naming God, just as each person has distinctive names and images to help them understand and relate to God. A few of the many:

Giver of Peace
Stealer of Hearts
Protector of the Poor
The One who carries everyone on her back
The Greatest of Friends
Architect of the World
Home of the World
The One who has not let us down yet
The One who spoke and the world was
Justice of the World
Peace of the World
The One who understands
The One who can turn everything upside down
The One who gives to all
The One who is heard in all the world
Destroyer of Fear
Holder of the Wheel of the Cosmos
Answerer of Prayers

*Images of God in personal life*

Several years ago octuplets were born to a Nigerian Christian couple in Houston, Texas. These devout parents, influenced by the images of God with which they grew up, gave their children names from their African tradition, which have the following meanings:

God is great

God is beautiful

God thinks of me

God knows my way

God has my life

God is my strength

God is my leader

God is merciful

Amid these various images and names for God (and many more than those mentioned here), we have only just begun our understanding of (and relationship with) God. St. Augustine, St. Thomas Aquinas, and other great thinkers developed arguments throughout the ages that help us to understand that it is reasonable to believe in God. There are limits, however, to what we can know about God from reason, from images, from names. "Even when he reveals himself, God remains a mystery beyond words" (*Catechism of the Catholic Church*, no. 230).

## Catholics and Evolution

As we reflect on God and creation, the topic of evolution often comes to mind. Evolution is a scientific theory that higher forms of life evolved from lower ones. This theory does not contradict or interfere with the truth of faith that God created everything.

In Pope John Paul II's *Message to the Pontifical Academy of Sciences on Evolution* on October 22, 1996, he stated: "Today…new knowledge has led to the recognition of more than one hypotheses in the theory of evolution. It is indeed remarkable that this theory has been progressively accepted by researchers following a series of discoveries in various fields of knowledge. The convergence, neither sought nor fabricated, of the results of work that was conducted independently is in itself a significant argument in favor of this theory."

Science and religion ask different kinds of questions; they look at the same truth from different points of view. There is strong evidence that the human body evolved from a lower form of animal life. At the same time, Catholics believe that this happened by a plan set in motion by the Creator. Human beings are not simply the result of chance.

When Catholics talk about evolution, they are referring only to the body, never to the soul. Science, however, is not concerned with the study of the soul. Science leaves that to religion and theology. The church teaches that God creates each soul directly and immediately.

For Catholics, there is no clash or conflict between church teachings and what science tells us about evolution. Both are meant to bring us the truth, and the truth is one. Thus, Catholics may and do accept the theory that the human body evolved.

## For Your Reflection and Conversation

- *How do memories from your childhood influence your experience of God as father and as mother?*

- *What was your earliest image of God? How has it changed as you have grown?*

- *Choose an image to finish the statement "God's love is like..." Why did you choose the image you did?*

- *Is "Father" the only personal word you can use for God or are there others?*

- *What is it about creation that leads you to think about God? Is there a time of the day or a season of the year when you are especially aware of God's creative power?*

- *Read Psalms 8 and 104. Close your eyes and think about the universe as astronomers now describe it to us. Picture yourself from some vantage point in space: you are a tiny human being on a tiny planet in the vastness of the universe. Thank and praise God for creation.*

- *How do you see yourself as a participant with God in the act of creation?*

- *If God created everything, where does evil come from?*

- *If God is almighty, do your actions matter?*

## As You Deepen your Prayer

*A prayer to learn the lessons of God's creation*
Creation teaches us about God; creation also teaches us
about ourselves. This Ute American Indian prayer calls us
to reflect on what we might learn from God's created Earth.

Earth, teach me stillness
    As the grasses are stilled with light.
Earth, teach me suffering
    As old stones suffer with memory.

Earth, teach me humility
    As blossoms are humble with beginning.
Earth, teach me caring
    As the mother who secures her young.

Earth, teach me courage
    As the tree which stands all alone.
Earth, teach me limitation
    As the ant who crawls on the ground.

Earth, teach me freedom
    As the eagle who soars in the sky.
Earth, teach me resignation
    As the leaves which die in the fall.

Earth, teach me regeneration
    As the seed which rises in spring.
Earth, teach me to forget myself
    As melted snow forgets its life.

Earth, teach me to remember kindness
   As dry fields weep with rain.

*Prayers on the mystery of God throughout our tradition*
These ancient prayers can be a comfort and a challenge as
we reflect on the mystery of God.

It is right and just to sing of you, to bless you, to
praise you, to thank you, to worship you—for You
are God—ineffable, inconceivable, invisible, incom-
prehensible, always existing and ever the same, You
and Your only begotten Son and Your Holy Spirit.
*(St. John Chrysostom)*

My Lord and my God, give me everything that
brings me closer to you. *(St. Nicholas of Flue)*

Creator of all things, true source of light and wisdom, lofty origin of all being, graciously let a ray of
your brilliance penetrate into the darkness of my
understanding. *(St. Thomas Aquinas)*

Let nothing disturb you.
Let nothing frighten you.
All things are passing
but God never changes.
Patience gains all things.
If you have God, you need
nothing else. *(St. Theresa of Ávila)*

Write your blessed name, O Lord,
Upon my heart,
There to remain so indelibly engraved,
That no prosperity, no adversity
Shall ever move me from your love.
*(Thomas à Kempis)*

Holy God, we praise thy name;
Lord of all, we bow before thee.
All on earth, thy scepter claim,
All in heaven above adore thee.
Infinite thy vast domain,
Everlasting is thy reign. *(hymn based on the fourth-century*
**Te Deum***)*

And his name shall be called
Wonderful, Counselor,
The Mighty God, the Everlasting Father,
The Prince of Peace. *(from the chorus of Handel's* **Messiah***)*

# "...and in Jesus Christ, his only Son, our Lord, who was conceived by the Holy Spirit, born of the Virgin Mary..."

A preschooler had a remarkable insight into Jesus' Incarnation, his becoming human for us. She exclaimed with delight, "I get it! Jesus is God's Show-and-Tell!"

This section of the Creed, which begins our beliefs about Jesus, is packed with mystery, awe, and many ramifications for our lives.

"Incarnation" is a word meaning "the putting on or taking on of flesh." Christians define the *Incarnation* as the union of divinity with humanity in Jesus Christ. It is the mystery of the Second Person of the Blessed Trinity becoming one of us, the mystery of Jesus Christ being God and Man.

Jesus is truly divine and truly human. He is not God

23

disguised as a human or God wearing a human mask. Jesus is one of us, with a human soul and body like ours. To all who knew him, he was the man Jesus. He got hungry and thirsty; he grew tired. Sometimes he was happy, sometimes sad. He knew fear, loneliness, and discouragement. He was one of us in all things except sin. Nevertheless, in becoming fully human, he did not stop being God.

The perfect union of humanity and divinity in Jesus raises almost endless questions. The *Catechism of the Catholic Church* summarizes the church's belief: "Jesus Christ possesses two natures, one divine and the other human, not confused but united in the one person of God's Son. Christ, being true God and true man, has a human intellect and will, perfectly attuned and subject to his divine intellect and divine will, which he has in common with the Father and the Holy Spirit. The Incarnation is therefore the mystery of the wonderful union of the divine and human natures in the one person of the Word" (nos. 481-483).

Many theologians today, without in any way overlooking Jesus' divine sonship and its integral place in a balanced understanding of Christian beliefs, would give special emphasis to Jesus' humanity. The Letter to the Hebrews tells us that Jesus was like us in all things but sin. This opens up a wide range of considerations about Jesus' life and the personal struggles he endured. For many people, this provides the opportunity to identify more closely with Jesus, since he was one of us and experientially knows the joys and sorrows of human life.

In the Creed we pray, "[God's] only Son." The phrase was meant to answer a heresy known as Gnosticism, which argued that out of the Supreme Deity emanated multiple lesser deities. The Creed asserted that God was One and that the relationship between God and Jesus was unique. Jesus was of God.

The phrase also meant to signal to a non-Christian world—accustomed to using "Son of God" to assert for their king a claim to divine origin—that here was a relationship more kingly but vastly different from the kings of the world. This God was not one among many, and this Jesus was not a politician pretending to be divine.

The Creed, then, asserts a unique bond. Jesus and God are intimates, and Jesus, the human one, stands as our invitation, our proof, that we can be the same; we, too, can be children of God.

The Creed calls Jesus "Lord." The angels' announcement in Luke 2:10-11 calls Jesus Messiah, Lord, and Savior.

The word *Messiah* is a Hebrew word meaning "anointed one." When this word was translated into Greek by the early Church, the word became *Christos,* and in English, *Christ.* Messiah was a very important word for the Jewish people of Old Testament times. It reminded them that kings, priests, and prophets were anointed with oil. They were waiting for someone to come to rule and be a great warrior. Jesus, however, never thought of himself this way and never called himself the Messiah.

In Old Testament times, the transcendent God, Yahweh, was referred to as the Lord. Substituting *Lord* for *Yahweh* was a sign of respect. So *Yahweh (God)* and *Lord* meant the same thing. Because Jesus was the Son of God—human and divine—he, too, was Lord.

Just like the word *Lord,* the word *Savior* was used in the Old Testament to describe God. The work of the Savior is to bring salvation to the world. *Salvation* means "to heal," or "to be made whole." In Luke 2:10–11 Jesus, whose very name means "God saves," is announced to all as the Savior of the world.

## To Continue your Journey of Exploration

### Historicity of the Person of Jesus

Are the faith statements of the New Testament our only source of knowing whether or not Jesus existed? No. There are a number of ancient historical sources that verify and support the existence of Jesus. Two of them are the writers Josephus and Tacitus.

One of the most famous non-biblical sources that refers to Jesus comes from Flavius Josephus, a Jewish historian who died at the end of the first century,. In volume 18 of his *Antiquities of the Jews*, he writes:

> At this time there appeared Jesus, a wise man....For he was a doer of startling deeds, a teacher of people who received the truth with pleasure. And he gained a following both among many Jews and among many of Greek origin....And when Pilate, because of an accusation made by the leading men among us, condemned him to the cross, those who had loved him previously did not cease to do so....And up until this very day the tribe of Christians, named after him, has not died out.

Among several pagan Roman writers, we can read the

words of the Roman historian Tacitus. He wrote about the great fire in Rome during the reign of the emperor Nero in AD 64. Nero was afraid of rumors that he had set the great fire himself. Tacitus wrote:

> To squelch the rumor, Nero created scapegoats and subjected to the most refined tortures those whom the common people called "Christians," hated for their abominable crimes. Their name comes from Christ, who, during the reign of Tiberius, had been executed by the procurator Pontius Pilate. Suppressed for the moment, the deadly superstition broke out again, not only in Judaea, the land which originated this evil, but also in the city of Rome. *(Annals 15, 44)*

## Catholic Teachings about the Person of Christ

In the early church, the following question arose: after the Incarnation, was Jesus two persons—a divine person and a human person? Or was he one person, and if so, a human person or a divine person? The followers of Nestorius, the bishop of Constantinople, mistakenly thought that Jesus was a human person in whom God was housed. This implied that Jesus was two persons: a divine person and a human person—like putting flowers in a vase (a divine person inside a human person).

To set things straight, Nestorius himself asked that a church council answer the question. The Council of Ephesus was called in AD 431. That council, as well as the Council of Chalcedon in AD 451, condemned any teaching that would split Christ into two persons. Ever since that time the church has clearly taught that Jesus is one person: a divine person with two natures (a divine nature and a human nature). At the Incarnation the second person of the Trinity took on a human nature, not another person.

## FOR YOUR REFLECTION AND CONVERSATION

- *What do you admire most about Jesus? How would you like to be like him?*

- *Christians believe that Jesus is God-made-man. If God became one of us, what does this tell you about God? About yourself?*

- *Which title of Jesus best answers for you the question "Who do you say I am?"*

- *What is your favorite gospel story about Jesus? What does it reveal about him? What might this choice be saying about your own image of Jesus?*

- *As you reflect on what the Creed says about Jesus, how do you answer Jesus' question to you: "Who do you say that I am?" Personally or as a couple or within your family or during catechetical sessions or at the beginning of adult parish meetings, take time to reflect and share one or more of these reflection starters.*

  » How do I *know* that Jesus loves me?

  » A question that I would like to ask Jesus is…

» I think Jesus' favorite name for me is…

» My favorite name for Jesus is…

» If Jesus were alive physically today, where would he live; what would he be doing; who would his friends be?

» Who do I know who acts like Jesus—in my family, in my church, in our country?

» What if I saw someone through Jesus' eyes? How would that person look?

» Read Matthew 19:13–15. If I had been there, what would I have said to Jesus?

» What do I think Jesus would like to have happen in our world by the year 2025? In my parish? In my family?

» Where do I look for Jesus?

» I wonder what makes Jesus sad…

» What advertising slogan would be a good description of Jesus?

» A compliment I think Jesus would give me is…

» If I asked Jesus to teach me to pray, he would say…

» What quality about Jesus do I admire most? Do I
have that quality?

» This is how I would describe Jesus to someone
who has never heard of him…

» My favorite gospel story about Jesus is…

» This is my image of Jesus' dream for our world…

### As You Deepen your Prayer

The following are ideas (among many) from the church's
tradition of prayer that focus our attention on Jesus, the
Son of God. Use them in your prayer life; find other prayers
that focus your prayer on various aspects of Jesus, his life, his
message, his relationship with us.

### The O Antiphons

The "O" Antiphons are prayed during the last seven days
of Advent (December 17-24) and are an expression of the
church's longing for the coming of Jesus:

O Wisdom, that proceeds from the mouth of the
Most High, reaching from end to end mightily, and
sweetly disposing all things: come and teach us the
way of prudence.

O Adonai, and Leader of the House of Israel, who
appeared to Moses in the burning bush and gave

him the Law of Sinai: come and redeem us by your outstretched arm.

O Root of Jesse, who stands as the emblem of the people, before whom kings shall not open their lips, to whom the Gentiles shall pray: come and deliver us; delay no more.

O Key of David, and Scepter of the House of Israel, who opens and no one shuts: come and lead the captive from the prison, and the one who sits in the shadow of darkness and in the shadow of death.

O Orient, Splendor of the eternal Light, and Sun of Justice: come and enlighten those who sit in darkness and in the shadow of death.

O King of the Gentiles, and their very desire, the Cornerstone that makes both one: come and save humanity, whom you have made out of the dust of the earth.

O Emmanuel, our king and lawgiver, the expectation of all the nations, and the Savior: come and save us, O Lord our God.

## Meditation (through Scripture passages)

God revealed divine love to us in the person of Jesus Christ, the Word made flesh. Jesus shared all our human characteristics and feelings. In the gospels we find a description of the human experiences of Jesus.

Select from the list below a story that describes a feeling or human characteristic of Jesus. Reflect on the meaning of this story. Use the questions that follow to assist you. You may wish to record your insights in a prayer journal.

Jesus as compassionate: Matthew 9:36
Jesus as angry: Matthew 21:12-13; Mark 3:5
Jesus as troubled: John 11:33
Jesus as tempted: Matthew 4:1-11
Jesus crying: John 11:35-36
Jesus as loving: Mark 10:21
Jesus as emotionally upset: Mark 14:32-42

- *With which human feelings of Jesus do you identify?*

- *How did Jesus handle these feelings?*

- *Knowing how Jesus handled these feelings, how will this— how might this—make a difference in your everyday life?*

# CHAPTER FOUR

# *"[He] suffered under Pontius Pilate, was crucified, died and was buried..."*

As we pray the Creed, we quickly move from the birth of Jesus to his suffering and death. There is no mention of his life, ministry, and teachings. To us, that seems very strange. Remembering, though, that the Creed was originally written as a defense against the heresies that plagued the early church, it does make sense. The framers of the Creed felt no need to affirm the life of Jesus because that was not being disputed. What was in dispute were the implications of Jesus' life and ministry. Therefore, the Creed focused on the death and resurrection of Jesus.

One of the things that stands out in this article of the Creed is the reference to Pontius Pilate. Pilate has the distinction of being the only person other than the Trinity and the Virgin Mary to be mentioned in the Creed by name. Why would this happen? Again, the original purpose of the Creed provides the answer. Among the heresies of the early church were some that disputed the death of Jesus (and, by implication, his resurrection) as historical reality.

The best way to refute this was to link the event to an actual historical figure.

As we look at the original words of the Creed—and their omission of a reflection on the life, ministry, and teachings of Jesus—it is important to remember that even though Jesus' death and resurrection are the key saving mysteries, we are indeed saved also by all the events of Jesus' life. (This also links our lives, our work, and our ministry more closely with his.)

Jesus' life was crucially important. The way a person dies punctuates his or her life. It was the life Jesus lived that led to the cross upon which he died. Jesus' death is an exclamation point of his profound love for us and of his unwavering obedience to the Father—the exclamation point to the way he lived his whole life. His death teaches us—calls us—to live as daughters and sons of God.

All of Jesus' life—each and every moment, each and every event—was critically and crucially important, not just the beginning and ending mysteries of his life. This is illustrated in the addition of the new mysteries of the Rosary, the Mysteries of Light, which commemorate five of the events of Jesus' ministry, whereas the Joyful, Sorrowful, and Glorious Mysteries, which we have meditated upon for centuries, all commemorate events at the beginning or ending of Jesus' life.

### …suffered under Pontius Pilate, was crucified,…

It seems that the element of the Creed that is the most straightforward and clear is the reality of life that is the most unclear: suffering. Yet, this may be the most important and consoling part of the Creed for many of us; for who has not confronted suffering in some form? What a consolation to know that Jesus, our brother, and the one we have chosen to follow, has suffered. What proof of his humanity!

## …died…

The giving of Jesus' life was total gift. There was no greater way Jesus could show his love for his Father. Jesus was the totally loyal son; he let the Father's love fill his life. Jesus was speaking of himself—and not just of his followers—when he said that one must die to live; one must lose in order to win (Mark 8:34–38). His love demanded that he give the greatest gift.

It's easy to see why we shy away from the cross. It's not that it's too painful; it's that it's too great a sign of love. We don't often love that fully, and we're embarrassed when God does. Our faith journey, it seems, is a gradual coming to accept the unbelievable tenderness of God. To be a follower of Christ is to die every day and rise every day.

For as we die, we rise. Salvation is letting Jesus bind us to himself. He is God and with God; he is human and with us. If the power of his cross is in us, we are, with him, lifted to new life (see, for example, the *Catechism of the Catholic Church*, no. 628).

## …and was buried;

We don't often concentrate a great deal on the burial of Jesus, yet it is significant. The Creed has three concise expressions regarding the death of Jesus: he was crucified, died, and was buried.

Perhaps this was done to confirm the reality of Jesus' death and to oppose the heresy of Docetism, which stated that Jesus had only an imaginary body, and therefore could not have really died. Against this view, Christians maintained that Jesus did actually die on the cross, and his body was laid in a tomb.

The gospel writers witnessed to the reality of death and burial of Jesus in various ways. In Mark (15:42ff) Joseph of Arimathea asks for the body of Jesus so he can bury it. (Ordinarily the bodies of people who were executed were not released to their relatives; they were buried in a common grave.) When Pilate was assured that Jesus was dead, he gave Joseph the right to remove the body.

In John (19:31ff) we find that Jesus, unlike the two thieves, has died on the cross. (Their legs were broken to hasten their death.) Jesus' side was pierced to be absolutely sure he was dead.

Around the year 55, preceding the writing of the gospels, Paul in 1 Corinthians 15:3–4 paves the way for these words of the Creed: "Christ died...he was buried."

## To Continue your Journey of Exploration

### The Teachings of Jesus

One of the reasons Jesus was crucified and put to death was because of the way he lived and how he taught. His teachings (the Good News) were too hard to hear for those in power—and perhaps for all hearers. (How would we have heard it? How do we hear it today?)

What are some of the main teachings of Jesus?

- The Reign of God is here. (Mark 4:1–20, 26–32)

- God is a loving Father. (Luke 11:1–13)

- God is merciful. (Luke 15:11–32)

- God's love is for everyone. (Matthew 22:1–14, 37-39; Luke 10:29–37)

- Repent, believe the good news, and imitate Jesus' life of service. (Luke 18:9–14; Matthew 25:31–46)

- The Lord is present in his church. (Matthew 28:20)

- The Lord is present through the Holy Spirit. (John 14:16–18, 25–26; 16:7–15)

- To accept Jesus is to accept the cross. (Luke 14:27)

Jesus' teachings, of course, encompass many challenges and all parts of our daily lives. The gospels also remind us that Jesus taught us key and critical life lessons on the following (in addition to many teachings): discipleship (Luke 9:23); love for our enemies (Matthew 5:44); faith (Luke 17:6); forgiveness (Matthew 18:21-22); how to live (Matthew 7:12); humility (Mark 10:31); judgment (Matthew 7:1); love (John 15:17); possessions (Luke 12:15); prayer (Matthew 7:7); sincerity (Matthew 6:1); true happiness (Luke 11:28); and worry (Matthew 6:33-34).

## For Your Reflection and Conversation

- *What would you say to someone who said that they could not understand why Jesus had to suffer and die before he rose?*

- *How does an awareness of the paschal mystery (Jesus' life, death, and resurrection) help you cope with disappointment, sickness, or loss? How could it, or has it, helped you comfort others in their suffering?*

- *What have you learned from your personal sorrows and sufferings?*

- *What opportunities have you had to share in another's suffering? What have you learned from their personal sorrows and sufferings?*

- *When bad things happen to good people, how do you respond to those who blame God for not interceding?*

- *The mystery of the cross is that "one must die to live; one must lose in order to win." Do you see that mystery present in your life? Have you or have others you know ever had to lose in order to win, to die in small ways in order to live?*

- *The actions of Jesus that eventually led to his crucifixion and death were loving, self-giving, and teaching of the Father's love. Think of a time when you were persecuted or crucified for living out your convictions. What was the result?*

- *Jesus taught not only through his words but through his ac-*

*tions. He taught mercy and compassion. Recall a time when you expressed mercy or compassion for another. What was painful, joyful, frightening, or powerful in your experience? What did you give up and what did you gain?*

- *Read Galatians 3:10–14. To "hang on a tree" made a Jew accursed, and the message that person taught would also have been accursed. How would this have made followers of Jesus feel after their leader was crucified?*

- *In what situations are we tempted to abandon those who suffer?*

- *Read the four passion narratives Matthew 26:1—27:66; Mark 14:12—15:47; Luke 22:1—23:56; John 13:1— 19:42) one scene at a time. What differences do you note in the way the action unfolds? What characters appear in each account? What impressions of Jesus emerge?*

## To ponder and live the story

Jesus calls his followers to pick up the cross and follow him. The Son of God picked up the cross of human suffering. Especially in Mark's gospel, the human Jesus accepted his cross—the cruelty and pain inflicted on him—without resisting. Reflect on the difference between accepting and taking up the cross.

- *What crosses have you accepted because of being a follower of Jesus?*

- *What crosses might you take up for the sake of others?*

- *As you look around the world—the world close to you, the wider world—what decision will you make to take up the cross of following Jesus for the sake of others?*

For Paul, raw, ugly suffering was the way our salvation was accomplished.

- *Volunteer to take the Eucharist to those who are suffering in the hospital or to those confined to their homes. Help them be aware that they are active members of the Body of Christ through their suffering.*

Spend some time with people who are suffering.

- *In addition to hospitals, nursing homes, and homeless shelters, you may find them in courtrooms, counseling centers, dining rooms, classrooms, finance meetings, cocktail parties, research labs, and your own home.*

Be alert to how your attitude toward suffering contributes to your daily responses.

How can you use various forms of communication and technology to voice your support or opposition to important issues of justice and human rights?

- *Decide on one concrete thing you can do yourself and with others.*

Since your mind and heart can go places your feet and hands cannot, in what ways do you think globally when you pray?

## As You Deepen your Prayer

- *Take a few moments this week to reflect on the words of one of the memorial acclamations we pray during the Eucharistic Prayer:* **Save us, Savior of the world, for by your cross and resurrection you have set us free.**

- *Read Galatians 2:19–21. Paul says that he has been crucified with Christ and now Christ lives in him. Think of the sorrows that you have had in your life. Pray that these unite you with Christ crucified. Realize that he lives in you.*

- *When putting your children or grandchildren to bed at night, sign them with the cross while saying, "Remember God loves you and so do I."*

- *Begin your day by slowly making the sign of the cross with a large gesture on your body as a reminder that all that you do that day is done in the name and under the care of our God.*

- *Meditating on the Cross*

  We adore you,
  O Christ, and we praise you
  because by your holy cross
  you have redeemed the world.

We pray this prayer often during the Stations of the Cross. The Stations help us to meditate on the meaning of the death and resurrection of Jesus.

On Good Friday, the church provides a ritual that also helps us to remember the paschal mystery. This ritual, the adoration of the cross, invites us to honor the cross in an act of love.

> Behold the wood of the Cross,
> on which hung the salvation of the world.
> Come, let us adore.

Pause for a few moments before a crucifix and pray one of these prayers.

# CHAPTER FIVE

# *"He descended into hell; on the third day he rose again..."*

Years ago, a rather prominent preacher and his wife were discussing the beauty of the Easter season. The wife was moved by the music, love, and joy of the season. As the camera zoomed in on her, she said to her husband, "At this time of year, everything seems to be coming to life. It feels so wonderful to be a Christian. I'd believe all of this even if it weren't true!"

The audience applauded.

St. Paul would not have tolerated such thinking. The resurrection of Jesus either happened or it didn't. Christianity either stood on reality or it didn't.

But first, as we come to the part of the Creed that proclaims the central mystery of our faith, the resurrection, we encounter the four words of the Creed that may be hardest to understand, "he descended into hell."

Perhaps it is helpful to remember that we have two primary creeds in the church. The Nicene Creed—an expanded creed coming from church councils, which clearly articulated church teaching and belief—says that Jesus died, was buried, and on the third day rose.

In the earliest versions of the Apostles' Creed, there was no mention of the phrase "he descended into hell." This was added later, with the English translation going back and forth between "descended into hell" and "descended to the dead."

With the liturgical changes to the Roman Missal (Advent 2011), the wording was changed to "he descended into hell; on the third day he rose again from the dead…"

These two clauses, of course, are very connected. They also call us to understand them through religious meaning, rather than the popular culture. "Hell," in popular meaning, has become a place of demons and punishment for evil people. In the biblical world, "hell" is the scriptural description for the place of all the dead.

When we look at the icons of the resurrection from our Eastern Tradition, they show the "gates of hell" falling away into the shape of a cross. Through dying, Christ has destroyed death. Because of that, he has changed the fate of all those who died before the crucifixion. In rising from the dead, Christ takes the dead with him.

In praying these words, we profess our belief that Christ is Lord for all ages—that his saving work is not just about us but about everyone.

The resurrection of Jesus from the dead is the bedrock truth of our faith. It is the heart of the good news about Jesus. The conviction that Jesus was a living presence after death is so central that St. Paul said, "If Christ has not been raised, then our proclamation has been in vain and your faith has been in vain" (1 Corinthians 15:14).

What was the risen Jesus like? Exactly how did the disciples experience him? What seems certain yet mysterious in the gospel accounts is that Jesus was truly transformed through the resurrection. He was experiencing an utterly new kind of existence.

The resurrection of Jesus was not a resuscitation (as with Lazarus), nor a waking from deep sleep. Resurrected life is not merely a continuation after death of the kind of earthly life we experience. It is, rather, an entirely new way of living, a new relationship in and with God.

Christ's body was glorified; it was not confined by space or time. It was not a ghost. He could appear and disappear before their eyes. Closed doors did not bar him. His was a real body but glorified, not belonging to earth but to the Father's realm.

The angel's words to the women at the grave speak of an event that has no past or future, only a present. This is not true of all other human events; things happen and then pass into history. This is not true of the resurrection of Jesus. It is the event that lives forever.

This mystery of our faith says much about Jesus, but it doesn't end there. If it is true, if it is important and significant for our faith, it also says something about us. It says that we too are ready to be transformed. Because the new life of Jesus rises in us, we rise to new life as well.

In the resurrection, a new message was given to humanity. The human story is no longer birth, life, death, corruption. It is now—and will always remain—birth, life, death, and eternal life. The message of the resurrection is that our bodies, our entire lives, matter.

We certainly believe that our lives will share eternal life, new life, with God when we die, but this life also begins right now. The resurrection of Jesus calls us to a new way of living, a new way of seeing things *now*—a different way than the world sees, believes, and acts.

That is as revolutionary and challenging as the resurrection was for the apostles. Are we really aware of its meaning and ready to live all of its implications?

## *To Continue your Journey of Exploration*

### The Proclamation of the Resurrection throughout Christianity

The centrality of the resurrection can be seen in all of the Christian religions. To look at just one example: for the Zairean Christian, this proclamation of faith is found often in their worship service and expresses for them the kernel— the very core—of their (and our) confessional faith:

**Leader**: Yesu Azali Na Bomoli!! *(Jesus has Life!!)*

**Congregation** (shouting): Hallelujah!! Yesu Azali Na Bomoli!!

**Leader**: Hallelujah!! *(thus completing the circle or exchange)*

The profound double meaning of this Lingala phrase is that of:

- *Jesus has Life (Jesus is alive); the equivalent of our Easter proclamation of "He is risen!"*

- *Jesus has life (to offer). Jesus has in his possession (your) eternal life.*

This is the message of grace in salvation. Quite literally, this call to worship or affirmation in praise has also taken on an existential reality during their troubled days. As the Israelites in the desert depended on God for daily manna, so, too, Zaireans see themselves as totally dependent on the church of Jesus Christ for any future life or resurrection of their developing country.

## Resurrection in the Gospels

Curiously, the gospel accounts of the resurrection are brief compared with those of the final days of Jesus' life. Each evangelist offers his own version of what happened. They have these points in common:

- *Various people go to the tomb and discover that the body of Jesus is no longer there.*

- *The people who go to the tomb find out—either on their own (in John's gospel) or through one or more messengers of God (in the synoptic gospels)—that Jesus is no longer dead but alive, and that he will reveal himself to them again soon.*

- *The initial reactions of the witnesses are, quite naturally, shock and then fear. But soon they experience Jesus among them in such striking ways that there can be no doubt it is he—alive again, and yet somehow very different from when he walked among them before his death.*

## Some Things We Learn from Christ's Resurrection

- *If Jesus had not risen, our faith would mean nothing.*

- *God acts in the world.*

- *It was an affirmation of the truth of Jesus' teachings.*

- *In light of the resurrection, suffering and the cross have meaning.*

- *Resurrection demonstrates the divinity of Jesus.*

- *Resurrection and ascension complete the paschal mystery.*

- *Through the paschal mystery, we are offered salvation and divine life.*

- *How we live here matters.*

- *Jesus' resurrection is the principle and source of our bodily resurrection.*

## Reflecting on the Emmaus Story

The story of what happened to the two disciples on the road to Emmaus is an intriguing incident. Some Scripture scholars suggest the two disciples are husband and wife. They are filled with the anxieties and disappointments of the day. They are immersed in the events of their world and can't figure out why everyone else isn't. "Are you the only one around," they ask the stranger who joins their company, "who hasn't heard about what's happened in Jerusalem in these days?"

They are engulfed in their own world and overwhelmed by its problems. Aren't we all frequently?

Jesus helps them see the problems of their life and the events of their world in the light of Scripture. He gives them a vision of life from God's point of view. They become excited about the different view this gives them of the reality they're experiencing. However, they do not recognize Jesus yet.

They offer Jesus hospitality. Then they come to recognize Jesus in the breaking of the bread. This is the bread of hospitality, but it also has overtones and alludes to the Bread of Eucharist.

It is by meeting with another, by being open and receptive, and by offering the bread of hospitality that they come to recognize the risen Lord.

It's very interesting to see what the two disciples do after they have recognized Jesus in the breaking of the bread and he disappears: they return to Jerusalem.

They are converted, literally, "turned around." They go back to tell the others of their experience of the risen Lord. They join the others who will spend the rest of their lives witnessing to the risen Lord. They spread the good word— Christ is risen!

Jesus did not return to life. Lazarus returned to life, his old life, a continuation of his former life. Jesus rose to new life, a different kind of life, related to his former life, undoubtedly, as the scars and the prints of the nails and the spear showed, but far superior to his life before the crucifixion.

Resurrection is meant to startle us and turn us around. We can get bogged down in this world and its challenges. We think we must have it all here. Is that why, at times, we find it hard to share what we have and get by with a little less so that those with nothing can have something?

The Emmaus incident models the structure and celebration of our liturgy. First we have the Liturgy of the Word where an account of God's relationship with God's people is proclaimed and the homily applies that word of God to today's life. We then celebrate the Liturgy of the Eucharist where we share not just the bread of fellowship and hospitality but the very Bread of Life.

Each week, do we expect to leave liturgy the same as we went in? Are we open and receptive? Are we willing to be converted? Turned around? Do we realize that in celebrating Eucharist we are called to change, to become ever more the Body of Christ?

Do we take time to offer hospitality, companionship, and friendship to those we encounter—and those we don't see across the globe—on our journey through life? Is this the message of the resurrection? If we truly heard this message, would we have more awareness of the presence of the risen Lord in all the moments of our daily lives? Is this the challenge of the resurrected Jesus and his call to us to be his effective witnesses in a world that is hurting and in need of peace and healing?

## Reflections on Puzzling Elements in the Resurrection Stories

In all the appearances of the risen Lord, there are some common elements that have meaning. They are often dismissed as merely puzzling. Some thoughts on possible meanings:

### *Why don't people recognize Jesus right away?*

Mary Magdalene mistakes Jesus for the gardener. The disciples on the road to Emmaus don't recognize him until the breaking of the bread. Thomas wasn't going to take anyone's word that Jesus had risen.

They were seeing Jesus but not in the usual sense of seeing. They were not seeing Jesus in the strictly scientific, historical, physical sense. They were experiencing Jesus really and truly and seeing him in a sense, in a true sense but in a different sense. They were seeing him with the eyes of faith.

### *What is the significance of "eating"?*

In all the resurrection appearances, "eating" happens. On the seashore with the disciples in Galilee, Jesus barbecues a few fish. Jesus eats in the Emmaus episode and in at least one other appearance—when he upbraids the disciples for being afraid and thinking that he's a ghost. He tells them to touch him and eats a bit of fish in their presence. Why?

He's real. He's really there. It's no dream or mirage. But might it also mean that we go along our way with our companions and don't get to know them because we don't break the bread of fellowship with them? We don't let ourselves descend (or really ascend) to a level of intimacy that enables us to see in them the Lord.

Also, having a little snack, a bite to eat, is a very human thing. Perhaps the problem with the years of Jesus' physical life on earth was that he seemed so human that people couldn't believe he was God. Now, in his risen state, it is tremendously important that people remember that he is human. His eating a few bites now and then is a way of affirming the Incarnation. The resurrection doesn't mean that finally Jesus went back to being God again. He never ceased being God. But he never ceases being human.

Eating is a simple action. It is very ordinary. We who are witnesses to the risen Lord have to look for his presence in the ordinariness of our own lives. Even more, we have to bring the risen Lord to the ordinary parts of the life we share with others in a way that seems natural and normal— like eating.

### Why does the risen Lord still bear the marks of the wounds?

Life is a continuum. The next life is not something completely separated from this life. The risen Jesus was in continuity with, but not exactly identical with, the Jesus who lived before and endured the cross. The wounds caused by the nails and the spear became emblems of victory. They have meaning now, but their meaning has been transformed. Our sufferings will continue to have meaning too, for all eternity.

### Why don't more people encounter the risen Lord? Perhaps a related question: Why don't we encounter the risen Lord more often?

In one of the gospel episodes, the women come to the tomb and find "two men in dazzling garments" who ask them, "Why do you seek the living among the dead?"

The same question might be addressed to us. Perhaps we

don't look for the risen Lord in the right places. We think that the less human we become, the more like God we become. That the more "celestial" we try to be, the closer to God we will get. We do more looking than doing. Perhaps we don't look with faith. Perhaps we've driven the risen Lord out of our world. Have we confined him to prayerful settings and quiet places? Certainly, God is there in the quiet of the church; but God is also elsewhere. God is in the busyness of business and in the small moments, the ordinary moments and actions of everyday life, if we but just look with faith and recognize.

## For Your Reflection and Conversation

- *In what areas of your life and relationships are you now experiencing new life after a time of struggle and loss? Do you allow yourself to be surprised? Do you surprise others in loving ways?*

- *What new configurations of thoughts, attitudes, and actions seem required in your life as a result of your faith in the risen Christ?*

- *Is your faith and hope in the risen Christ the foundation of your peace, despite your struggles and suffering?*

- *If you take a few minutes to reflect on (or be with) Mary as she encounters the risen Lord, what words burst forth from you at such a graced moment?*

- *Does the Lord's presence in your life cause your heart to "burn within" you as the disciples experienced on the way to Emmaus? Where do you direct this passion?*

- *Why do we speak of Jesus' death-resurrection as a "combined event"? In what way is Jesus' death-resurrection the world starting over? Have you ever known a starting over in your life? Does your experience of Jesus' death-resurrection provide a starting over for you?*

- *What does Jesus' resurrection say about the relationship between God and human beings?*

- *Reflect on the ways you experience dying and rising as a part of your daily life. Some examples might be: sleeping and waking, learning something new and "dying" to your former ignorance, saying goodbye and hello, watching the seasons change, going from messy to clean, illness, moving, etc.*

- *After the resurrection, Jesus had to give the disciples the power to recognize him, to know him again. Does this process of recognizing Jesus go on today? Has this happened in your own life?*


### As You Deepen your Prayer

### The Memorial Acclamation

During liturgy we proclaim our belief in the paschal mystery through the memorial acclamation. As you reflect in the coming days on the resurrection, use these acclamations as a part of your prayer:

We proclaim your Death, O Lord,
and profess your Resurrection
until you come again.

When we eat this Bread and drink this Cup,
we proclaim your Death, O Lord,
until you come again.

Save us, Savior of the world,
for by your Cross and Resurrection
you have set us free.

## Suggestions for Journaling Prayer

- *Where are the instances of resurrection in your life?*

- *How have you been surprised by a turn of events that has opened a new path for you when you thought that things were hopeless? How have you shared the resurrection that you have received?*

- *What are the things and places, and who are the people in your life, that you would like to experience resurrection?*

- *What ways have you tried or do you try to promote resurrection to others?*

- *The women at the tomb were asked, "Why do you seek the living among the dead?" Are you being asked the same question?*

- *Are you looking for the risen Lord in the right places? Have you confined the Lord only to church or only to the places where you think he should be? Are you missing him other places?*

- *Have you also confined God to only the "hard things" in your life by only going to God in prayer when things are hard? Do you go to God during the joyful times, also?*

- *If you only go to God during the difficult times, does this lead you to see God as a punishing God? Do you see God everywhere, especially in all the good things that happen (or do you take credit for the good things)?*

# CHAPTER SIX

# *"He ascended into heaven, and is seated at the right hand of God...from there he will come to judge the living and the dead."*

## "He ascended into heaven..."

Years ago I asked a friend why he thought we didn't celebrate the Ascension more enthusiastically. His reply was because it didn't fall on a Sunday (now, years later, many of us do celebrate it on a Sunday), and no one gets any presents. It sounded funny at the time, but recently, reflecting on the meaning of the Ascension, I realize it's a "more-than-worth-celebrating" feast of our faith.

The feast of the Ascension is all about the presence, not the absence, of Jesus. The apostles did not understand the ascension to mean that Jesus was no longer with them. They expressed no grief or disappointment. Instead, they "returned to Jerusalem with great joy" (Luke 24:52). That's not the emotion you feel when you lose your best friend. The ascension did not mean they lost something. They gained something. Jesus' ascension brought him closer to them and to us than he was before. He left us on that mountain so that he might be with us in California, Washington, DC, Israel and Iraq, etc. He was taken from our physical sight so that he might come to us—everyone—wherever we are.

The Ascension is not about absence; it's about presence. Jesus told us, "I will be with you all days even to the end of the world." The words of the third Eucharistic Prayer for Masses with Children (spoken to God the Father) proclaim this clearly: "Jesus now lives with you in glory, but he is also here on earth, among us."

Thus, this mystery of the Ascension makes a difference to us:

Jesus told his disciples that in order for the Holy Spirit to come, he had to return to the Father. The rather limited physical presence of Jesus (which could only be shared by a few disciples) had to be withdrawn so that the universal presence of Jesus might become available forever to everyone all over the world.

Second, the Ascension tells us finally and completely who Jesus really is. The picture of Jesus returning to God the Father enables us to let go of previous and incomplete pictures of Jesus. Certainly Jesus is the baby at Bethlehem, but that's not who he is now. He is the teacher of the Sermon on the Mount, but we know much more than just a record of his words. He died on the cross, but that's not where he is today. Ascension adds a final and critical photograph to the album of who Christ is and what he does. He is ascended—once more with the Father, Lord of Heaven and

Earth, Ruler of Life and Conqueror of Death, the ruler of all human history. Jesus is alive and well and is still active every day. It's much more important that we see what Jesus *is* doing, than worrying about what he "would" do.

And third, Jesus' ascension gives us something to do. Jesus commanded the apostles (and us) to make disciples of all nations, teaching them to obey his commandments. With one stroke, Jesus removed any and all ethnic and racial barriers. All people of all nations are to be invited and are to share in the communion of the church. There is also to be no barrier between the apostles and their converts, for all commandments apply to all people.

### "...he will come to judge the living and the dead."

Judgment has always been a core belief of our faith. We believe that Christ will come to us when we die, and we will be judged at that moment. The full meaning of our lives, however, will not be complete until the world ends. For example, as a parent, a teacher, a social worker, etc., we may have a significant impact on one—or many—lives. Those people, in turn, may help others, resulting in much good through the ages. At the same time, an evil life can have repercussions that last through many centuries. So, at the end of time, Jesus will bring human history to a close in a final judgment, which will not change the results of the particular judgment but will bring the consequences of our deeds to light.

Often, judgment strikes fear in our hearts. The Jewish people—who shaped our faith centuries ago—saw law as a blessing and never thought of judgment as condemnation. Thus, the segment of our Creed about judgment is not a call to fear but a call to growth, to faithfulness to Jesus and his lifestyle. We have been created not only for heaven on judgment day but to bring with us what we have done to build the Reign of God. The judgment of humanity has something to do with having left the world better than when we first received it. God waits for us to continue the re-creating work of Jesus Christ, which will only be completed when he comes again.

## To Continue your Journey of Exploration

### Ascension in the New Testament

What do the various books of the New Testament share with us about the Ascension?

*The Gospels of Matthew and John:* No account of a visible ascension.

*The Gospel of Mark:* On Easter Sunday, Jesus appeared first to Mary Magdalene, then to two disciples on a country road (these appearances are not described). Jesus then appears to the eleven at table and commissions them to go into the whole world and proclaim the gospel. Then there is a visible ascension: "So then the Lord Jesus, after he spoke to them, was taken up into heaven and took his seat at the right hand of God" (Mark 16:19).

*The Gospel of Luke:* A visible ascension takes places on Easter Sunday. The disciples were gathered together talking about appearances that had already taken place that day. In the midst of this, the Lord appeared, spoke, and ate with them. The visible ascension follows: "Then he led them out as far as Bethany, raised his hands, and blessed them. As he blessed them he parted from them and was taken up to heaven" (Luke 24:50–51).

*The Acts of the Apostles*: Here, Luke gives another account of the ascension (Acts 1:1–11), which indicates that Jesus appeared to the disciples "during forty days."

Christ's death, resurrection, ascension, and sending of the Spirit were really all parts of a single event, each one flowing out of the other. In our liturgical celebration of this mystery, we spread it out over many weeks so that we can take it all in, which is what Luke did in Acts: after Easter Sunday, Jesus appears at different times over forty days; then he visibly ascends to heaven. Ten days later, there is the dramatic outpouring of the Spirit at Pentecost.

What this means for each of us and for the church is so great that we need time to digest it all: we need the fifty days of the Easter season.

## The Candle Remains Lit

Years ago (prior to the renewal of the liturgy that came about because of the Second Vatican Council), in many places a small ritual was observed during the Mass of Ascension Thursday. The ritual became part of our observance probably because the full meaning of the Ascension was not understood, or had become obscured throughout the years.

After the story of the ascension had been proclaimed in the gospel, the paschal candle—a symbol of the risen Jesus with us—was extinguished. The message that it gave us was that Jesus had ascended; he was now gone from us.

That no longer happens. We have returned to a more accurate understanding of the ascension. The ascension is a new form of human existence that enables Jesus to transcend the barriers of time and space and, through his Spirit, be present with us, with all of creation, in every time and place. The ascension of Christ is not about absence; it is about presence.

## A Parable

After Jesus ascended into heaven, all the angels raced around to meet him and to hear how things had gone. Jesus told them about his birth, his life and preaching, his death and resurrection, and how he had saved the world.

And the angels said, "Well, now that you are back here, how is your work going to be continued? What is your plan?"

And Jesus said, "Well, I gathered a group of people who believe in me and love me, a group of human beings, and they're going to continue the gospel and the church."

The angels looked at him in shock and then said, "Well, what will you do if that doesn't work? What are your other plans?"

And Jesus said, "I have no other plans."

*We're it! There are no other plans.*

## FOR YOUR REFLECTION AND CONVERSATION

- *How do you think the apostles felt after the ascension? Did they experience the absence of Jesus or the presence of Jesus?*

- *What is "presence"? Do you feel Jesus' absence or his presence?*

- *Have there been times when you've stayed looking up at the clouds rather than looking for Jesus in the here and now?*

- *What is the mission that Jesus left for you?*

- *The ascension is about spectators and witnesses. When are you a spectator in your faith life? When are you a witness?*

- *How do you celebrate the feast of the Ascension? How does your parish celebrate it? How could you celebrate it?*

- *"It's a lot more important that we see what Jesus is doing than worrying about what he would do." How would that make a difference in our lives, in the life of our world?*

- *What are some of the challenges of the ascension for you, for your parish, for the church?*

- *When you think about judgment day, what feelings and thoughts come to mind?*

- *What are the good works that you are taking with you to judgment day? Do you think there might be people whom you have touched that you're not aware of?*

## As You Deepen your Prayer

These prayers—in the spirit of the message of the Ascension—may be prayed at home by families or in parish gatherings, as we recall the challenge of Jesus' call to us to preach and live the Good News.

Response to intentions: *Gracious God, set us on fire with your good news.*

Let us pray for all Christians everywhere who are called to preach the gospel. For this, let us pray to the Lord. R.

Let us pray for all church leaders and ministers, who encourage and lead us in the ministry of evangelization, for _____. For them, let us pray to the Lord. R.

Let us pray for those who preach the gospel by working for justice and peace. For them, let us pray to the Lord. R.

Let us pray for all those who preach the gospel in cultures that are not their own, that they may minister with sensitivity and respect for the gifts already given to the people among whom they live. For them, let us pray to the Lord. R.

Let us pray that all Christians may be enflamed with courage and creativity to be and preach the good news. For this, let us pray to the Lord. R.

# CHAPTER SEVEN

# "I believe in the Holy Spirit..."

What is the work of the Holy Spirit? The Holy Spirit empowers us to

witness more effectively
think more clearly
feel more deeply
listen more insightfully
speak more truthfully
love more extravagantly
care more ardently
serve more creatively
give more lavishly
encourage more lovingly
live more fully
teach more eloquently
participate more generously
pray more faithfully
worship more deeply
celebrate more joyfully

It is often said that the Holy Spirit is the forgotten person of the Holy Trinity. The more I think about it, especially reflecting upon some of the nudgings of the Spirit among us listed above, I don't think that is exactly the situation. Perhaps the real situation is that there is so much to say about the Spirit that we don't know how to put it into words.

## How Do We Explain "Spirit" and the Holy Spirit?

What is school spirit, team spirit? If a person is said to bring spirit to a group, what does that mean? Perhaps words like commitment, comfort, energy, or enthusiasm come to mind.

The word "spirit" is a translation of the Hebrew word for "breath," "air," or "wind," suggesting the vital role the Holy Spirit plays in our lives. This invisible Spirit is life-giving, life-sustaining, fresh, creative, mysterious, unpredictable, and uncontainable. The Holy Spirit is the Giver of Life, the breath of God's life, as essential as air is for our physical life.

The early church used several titles to remind the followers of Jesus of the identity and work of the Spirit. A few:

- *Advocate* (John 14:16): one who speaks on our behalf, defends us, comforts and consoles us

- *Spirit of truth* (John 14:17): one who communicates God's truth, inspires the Scriptures, guides our faith journey

- *Spirit of glory* (1 Peter 4:14): one who urges us on to the glory God has in store for us and who gives us the courage to share in Jesus' mission

## How Do We Know the Spirit's Presence in Our world?

We see the effects of the Spirit's work—what the Spirit has "left behind." We need only look for that which is true, beautiful, good, and honorable in creation, ourselves, and others. Every good deed ever done, every kindness ever offered, every moment of compassion, every hand held out in friendship, every act of justice, every work of peace is a visible sign of the Spirit in our world.

Perhaps it is best to sum up the Spirit's presence in two main categories. First, we encounter the Spirit in human relationships, especially love relationships. Romans 5:5 says, "God's love has been poured into our hearts through the Holy Spirit." Our prayer expresses, "Come, Holy Spirit, fill the hearts of your faithful, and kindle in them the fire of your love." Evelyn Underhill has noted: "To be unloving is to be out of touch with God." Turn that around, and to be loving is to be filled with the Holy Spirit, the Spirit of love.

Second, we encounter the Spirit in the building up of society. Our prayer continues, "Send forth your Spirit and they shall be created; and you shall renew the face of the earth." That may refer to the world of nature, but today we know that our social world needs renewal also. In today's world, there are many people and organizations, moved by the Spirit, who are working for peace and justice.

## Who/How is the Holy Spirit in Our Lives?

Throughout the church's history, we have used many symbols (fire, tongues of fire, anointing, hand, the seal, the finger of God, wind, dove, water, cloud, and light) to answer that question. Perhaps another might remind us of the Spirit's work through us. The Spirit is like the parent whose child is sitting on her or his lap blowing out birthday candles. The parent blows gently while the young child blows. The parent doesn't blow until the child blows. They are working together.

The Spirit has given us the gifts and works through us and with us, but we have to do our part, to use the gifts in building the Reign of God. No one else has the gifts in the same way we do, and the Spirit can't do it without us. Some ask the question, "Have you received the Holy Spirit?" Perhaps the question should be, "Does the Holy Spirit have you?"

## To Continue your Journey of Exploration

### The Holy Spirit Reveals God's Presence with Us

The *Catechism of the Catholic Church* (no. 688) sets out seven ways in which the Holy Spirit provides us with an experience of God's presence.

- When we pray and study the Scriptures, which the Spirit inspired, we can sense God's presence in the biblical words.

- When we read the lives of the saints, their teachings and witness, we can be motivated to holiness by their example, which was shaped by the Spirit.

- When we assent with obedience to the teachings of the Magisterium, we are guided by the Spirit. The Spirit's presence is noticeably experienced at ecumenical councils.

- When we actively participate in the liturgies and sacraments of the church, we enter into a unique situation where the Spirit opens us to experience God, especially in the Eucharist.

- When we give ourselves to prayer, whether that is the Liturgy of the Hours or the Rosary or meditation, or any form of prayer, we join the Holy Spirit who prays with us and intercedes for us.

- When we offer ourselves to the various apostolates of the church, we have the Spirit providing us with the confidence and energy we need.

- When we dwell on the Great Tradition of the Church, its marvelous history and a host of saintly witnesses, we sense the Spirit's sustaining power through it all.

## The Seven Gifts of the Holy Spirit

The prophet Isaiah (11:1–2) speaks about the Messiah (Anointed or Christ) who will possess the fullness of the Spirit and his sevenfold gifts. Jesus reveals to us in the discourse beginning his public life in the synagogue at Nazareth: "The Spirit of the Lord is upon me, for he has anointed me..." (Luke 4:18).

The very word "Christ" means "Anointed One." The Father is the One who anoints, Christ is the One who is anointed, and the anointing is the Holy Spirit. We, as baptized Christians, share in the anointing of Christ, the Anointed One. At baptism we receive the seven gifts of the Holy Spirit; at confirmation we are united more closely to Christ and these seven gifts are increased in us.

The *Catechism of the Catholic Church* (no. 1831) tells us: "The seven gifts of the Holy Spirit...complete and perfect the virtues of those who receive them. They make the faithful docile in readily obeying divine inspirations."

- *Wisdom:* the ability to see things from all sides, to get the "whole picture." True wisdom is not just learning facts but seeing the relationship among the facts. This gift helps us see that there is another viewpoint or vision of the world—God's. (Wisdom 7:12-14; Sirach 1:1; 14:20-27; Proverbs 2:1-6)

- *Understanding:* the ability to see from another person's "heart," to feel the feelings of others and to put these before our own. This gift enables us to "stand under" or to gain deeper insight into what we believe by faith. Understanding is accepting others as they are and caring for the people no one else notices. (Wisdom 3:9; Proverbs 24:3)

- *Knowledge:* the gift of objectivity, of seeing the world and things around us as they really are, rather than as we would like them to be. This gift broadens our minds and hearts so that when we come together we can learn and share with one another. We know who we are as children of God by sharing together in worship, instruction, and prayer. Knowledge helps us to discover new and creative ways to meet needs. (Proverbs 19:27; 24:3–5)

- *Fortitude* or *Courage:* the ability to follow our convictions and conscience no matter what the cost. Courage gives us the strength to do what is right in spite of obstacles and difficulties. This gift frees us to live firmly by faith instead of by fear. (Psalm 118:6; 118:13–14; Philippians 1:12–14)

- *Counsel:* the gift of right judgment, the ability to make good decisions after looking at the alternatives and considering the consequences. It allows us to see a situation clearly, view the options, and make a clear choice. It also allows us to seek advice from those who have more experience. Sometimes this takes place in the sacrament of reconciliation. At other times the gift of counsel reaches us through other Christians who are ready to listen to our problems and help us. (Sirach 32:16–19; 37:7–15; Proverbs 15:22)

- *Piety* or *reverence:* the ability to treasure life and all that sustains it. Reverence helps us see the value of every person and thing God has created. This gift frees us to reverence and praise God in our worship and prayer life. It also helps us see God's holiness reflected in other people and in nature. (Psalm 118:23–24; 118:29; Sirach 42:15–25; 43)

- *Wonder and Awe in God's Presence (Fear of the Lord):* the ability to be amazed by things in life, to be awake to the realization that we are always in God's presence. The gift of wonder and awe tells us that God created the beauty of the universe but also listens to us, cares for us, and loves us beyond all measure. (Isaiah 29:23; Sirach 32:13; 43:28–33)

## The Twelve Fruits of the Holy Spirit

The fruits of the Holy Spirit show the effects of the Spirit's gifts to us. Just as a fruit tree produces fruit when properly nourished and cared for, people who make use of the Spirit's gifts show concrete evidence of their faithfulness.

- *Kindness:* the strength of Christ's love, which leads us to a greater service to others

- *Joy:* the ability to celebrate life even in the midst of pain and confusion because of deep, spiritual reservoirs

- *Peace:* quiet, inner confidence in God's care of my life that keeps me from feeling uptight and anxious

- *Patience:* a staying power that enables us to handle frustration and conflict without becoming unduly edgy or annoyed

- *Goodness and Generosity:* a real desire to live a holy life, to set a good example by my conduct wherever I am

- *Long-Suffering (positive attitude):* because we know we are loved, whole and complete with God's extraordinary gift, we are able to put up with the injuries, slights, and outrages of life

- *Humility:* an inner strength that permits me to be gentle in my relationships, open, and aware of my own abilities without having to make a show of them

- *Faith/Fidelity:* the ability to stick to my work; I can be counted on to stay firm in my commitment to God and to God's people with whom I am connected

- *Modesty:* because the Spirit of Love fills our life, we no longer need to impress other people with our power or degrees or connections or wealth

- *Self-Control:* learning to discipline my time, energy, and desires to reflect my spiritual values and priorities

- *Chastity:* the ability to form loving and caring friend-ships, which help us to act appropriately with our gift of sexuality

- *Love:* living by the priority of sensing the needs of the people with whom we work and live and respond as Jesus would

## With the Holy Spirit or Without the Spirit

The Eastern Church has usually been more aware of the Holy Spirit than we in the West. In one of their books, *Dialogues with Patriarch Athenagoras*, we read this splendid summary of the importance of the Holy Spirit:

"Without the Holy Spirit: God is far way,
Christ stays in the past,

the Gospel is a dead letter,
the Church is simply an organization,
authority a matter of domination,
mission a matter of propaganda,
the liturgy no more than an evocation,
Christian living a slave morality.

But in the Holy Spirit:
the cosmos is resurrected and groans
with the birth pangs of the Kingdom,
the risen Christ is there,
the Gospel is the power of life,
the Church shows forth the life of the Trinity,
authority is a liberating service,
mission is a Pentecost,
the liturgy is both memorial and anticipation,
human action is deified."

## FOR YOUR REFLECTION AND CONVERSATION

- *Can you remember an occasion when you said to yourself, "This is the Holy Spirit at work"?*

- *Is there a particular area in your life where you rely on the presence of God's Spirit? How do you know that this is the Holy Spirit at work within you?*

- *Have you ever felt surprised by how you dealt with a difficult situation? Did you attribute this to the Holy Spirit?*

- *Has there been a time in your life that you felt overwhelmed, wondered where your life was going, and discovered the Spirit at work within you?*

- *A song from the musical **Les Miserables** says, "To love another person is to see the face of God." Have you ever had that experience?*

- *What life experience have you had that you think was influenced by the presence of the Holy Spirit?*

- *Have you ever experienced a "conversion," a "transformation"? To what or whom do you attribute this experience?*

- *What do you need to say today to reveal that the Spirit is with you?*

- *What do these Scripture passages tell you about the work of the Spirit?*

  » The creation of humanity: Genesis 2:7

  » The story of Elijah in a cave: 1 Kings 19:9–13

  » Dry bones: Ezekiel 37:1–14

  » Pentecost: Acts 2:1–4

- *How does the Holy Spirit act to transform people's lives in the following Scripture passages?*

- » Acts 2:5–13

- » Acts 3:1–10

- » Acts 9:1–19

- » Acts 10:44–49

- *How has the Holy Spirit transformed your life?*

## Reflective Questions for the Gifts of the Holy Spirit

- *Fortitude: Think of a time when you managed to get through a difficult situation.*

- *Knowledge: Think of a time when you wanted to know the needs of another so that you could reach out and help.*

- *Understanding: Think of a time when you really listened to another's problem or when someone really heard what you were saying.*

- *Counsel: Think of a time when you tried to cheer up someone who was sad or suffering.*

- *Piety: What is your favorite way to pray?*

- *Fear of the Lord: When do you experience the closeness of God's presence?*

• *Wisdom: When has there been a time that you saw the big picture—not just your perspective but a focus on the common good, seeing things through God's eyes?*

## As You Deepen your Prayer

A Prayer based on Galatians 5 (The Fruits of the Spirit)

Holy Spirit, you lead us to love one another
in the way Jesus has first loved us.
Bless us, Holy Spirit, giver of Love.

Holy Spirit, in your presence we come to
know joy that will never end.
Bless us, Holy Spirit, giver of Joy.

Holy Spirit, you gift us with patience as we grow,
as we struggle,
and as we live together in community.
Bless us, Holy Spirit, giver of Patience.

Holy Spirit, you are kind to us.
Teach us to be kind to ourselves
and to one another.
Bless us, Holy Spirit, giver of Kindness.

Holy Spirit, you are generous in your presence with us
and generous in responding to our needs.
Teach us to be generous.
Bless us, Holy Spirit, giver of Generosity.

Holy Spirit, you reveal for us the faithfulness of our God.
Draw us to live more faithfully with you.
Bless us, Holy Spirit, giver of Fidelity.

Holy Spirit, you come to us in a gentle breeze.
Teach us to be gentle with ourselves and with one another.
Bless us, Holy Spirit, giver of Gentleness.

Lord, send us your Holy Spirit and fill our hearts with the fire of your love. Renew in us the gifts of your wisdom and compassion, your forgiveness and love, that we may serve as Jesus served.

## Litany of the Holy Spirit

A litany is a well-known and much appreciated form of responsive petition, used in public liturgical services and in private devotions.

The church has approved six litanies for public prayer; many new ones are frequently being written and prayed in private use. Today the litanies approved for public recitation are: All Saints, the Blessed Virgin, the Holy Name of Jesus, the Sacred Heart, St. Joseph, and the Most Precious Blood of Jesus Christ.

The following is a litany of the Holy Spirit for private use.

## A Litany of the Holy Spirit

Lord, have mercy on us.
Christ, have mercy on us.
Lord, have mercy on us.
Father all-powerful, have mercy on us.

Jesus, Eternal Son of the Father,
Redeemer of the world, save us.
Spirit of the Father and the Son,
boundless Life of both, sanctify us.

Holy Trinity, hear us.
Holy Spirit, Who proceeds from the Father and the Son,
enter our hearts.

Holy Spirit, Who is equal to the Father and the Son,
enter our hearts.
Promise of God the Father, have mercy on us.

Ray of heavenly light, *have mercy on us*
Author of all good,
Source of heavenly water,
Consuming Fire,
Ardent Charity,
Spiritual Unction,
Spirit of love and truth,
Spirit of wisdom and understanding,
Spirit of counsel and fortitude,
Spirit of knowledge and piety,
Spirit of the fear of the Lord,

Spirit of grace and prayer,
Spirit of peace and meekness,
Spirit of modesty and innocence,
Holy Spirit, the Comforter,
Holy Spirit, the Sanctifier,
Holy Spirit, Who governs the Church,
Gift of God the Most High,
Spirit Who fills the universe,
Spirit of the adoption of the children of God,

Holy Spirit, come and renew the face of the earth.
Holy Spirit, shed Your Light into our souls.
Holy Spirit, engrave Your law in our hearts.
Holy Spirit, inflame us with the flame of Your love.
Holy Spirit, open to us the treasures of Your graces.
Holy Spirit, teach us to pray well.
Holy Spirit, enlighten us with Your inspirations.
Holy Spirit, lead us in the way of salvation.
Holy Spirit, grant us the only necessary knowledge.
Holy Spirit, inspire in us the practice of good.
Holy Spirit, grant us the merits of all virtues.
Holy Spirit, make us persevere in justice.
Holy Spirit, be our everlasting reward.

Lamb of God, Who takes away the sins of the world,
send us Thy Holy Spirit.
Lamb of God, Who takes away the sins of the world,
pour down into our souls the gifts of the Holy Spirit.
Lamb of God, Who takes away the sins of the world,
grant us the Spirit of wisdom and piety.

Come, Holy Spirit! Fill the hearts of Your faithful,
and enkindle in them the fire of Your love.

Let us pray: Divine Spirit,
renew Your wonders in this our age as in a new Pentecost,
and grant that Your Church,
praying perseveringly and insistently with one heart
and mind
together with Mary, the Mother of Jesus,
and guided by Blessed Peter,
may increase the reign of the Divine Savior,
a reign of truth and justice,
a reign of love and peace.

Amen.

*(Prayer of Pope John XXIII in preparation for the Second Vatican Council.)*

## Prayer for the Seven Gifts of the Holy Spirit

Christ Jesus, before ascending into heaven, you promised
to send the Holy Spirit to your apostles and disciples.
Grant that the same Spirit may perfect in our lives the
work of your grace and love.

Grant us the Spirit of Wisdom that we may aspire to the
things that last forever;
the Spirit of Understanding to enlighten our minds with
the light of your truth;
the Spirit of Counsel that we may choose the surest way
of doing your will,
seeking first the Kingdom;

the Spirit of Fortitude that we may bear our cross with
  you and, with courage, overcome the obstacles that
  interfere with our salvation;
the Spirit of Knowledge that we may know you and know
  ourselves and grow in holiness;
the Spirit of Piety that we may find peace and fulfillment
  in the service of God while serving others;
the Spirit of Fear of the Lord that we may be filled with a
  loving reverence toward you.

Teach us to be your faithful disciples and animate us in
  every way with your Spirit. Amen.


## Come, Holy Spirit

Come, Holy Spirit,
fill the hearts of your people!
Help us, heal us, hold us in your love.
Mold us, meld us, make us your own.
Shake us, shape us, show us your truth.
Form us, free us, fill us with grace.
Defend us, mend us, send us your power.
Touch us, teach us, turn us to you.
Unite us, ignite us, delight us with joy.
Come, Holy Spirit,
fill the hearts of your people,
and renew the face of the earth!

# CHAPTER EIGHT

# *"[I believe in]...the holy catholic Church, the communion of saints..."*

Certain peoples of Zimbabwe in southern Africa greet each other by saying, "How are you?"

The response is, "I am well if you are well."

The first person then says, "I am well, so we are well."

What a commentary on that African tribe! That ritual says much about the next two sections of the Creed and what we pray: the unity of the church and all its members (its saints) living and dead and that our well-being is connected with each other.

## I believe in the holy catholic Church...

In the Nicene Creed we profess our belief in the four marks of the church: one, holy, catholic, and apostolic. The Apostles' Creed mentions only the "holy catholic Church."

These marks (or signs) are not only gifts given by God to the church, they are also tasks that we, the church, must constantly strive to bring about as God's people.

We believe in a church that is holy. By this we do not mean that the church has attained perfection. Rather, we mean that the church is an effective means of human holiness and wholeness. The sacraments nourish holiness, for example, even if the human beings who celebrate the sacraments are far from perfect. We believe in a church that is both holy and sinful. We are imperfect, and we are the church, so the church is imperfect, always in need of repentance and reform.

We believe in a church that is *catholic*. This word, first used in reference to Christians by St. Ignatius of Antioch around AD 100, means "universal" or "all-inclusive" and refers to Christ's church throughout the world. To believe in such a church is to believe that anything good, true, or beautiful is welcome in this church that we are. Our doors are wide open to all people; and as God's people we go into the world to bring the message of God's love to all people.

The Creed calls us to believe in a church that is *holy*. The church is holy when it is with the poor, with the outcast, with the forgotten. The church is holy when it makes holiness its reason for existence. It calls us to more than humanness, more than material world. It reveals the goodness of God, the sacredness of ordinary life, by making all of life holy at every turn. That is what we do in our sacraments, and the catholic sacramental principle is that all life, all creation, is holy.

The Creed calls us to believe in a church that is catholic, universal: a group of believers who embrace the whole world and rejects no one. The Catholic Church says "Here comes everybody" and really means it.

## I believe in the communion of saints…

People who need people: that is what we proclaim—our interdependence—when we pray this portion of the Creed. And rightly so, for that is how God created us. We are not saved as individuals. We go to God together or we don't go at all.

The doctrine of the communion of saints flows from our belief that we Christians are closely united as one family in the Spirit of Jesus. "Saints" in the Creed means not just those who have been canonized by the church but all God's holy people (*Catechism of the Catholic Church*, no. 946). All who are in Christ have been made holy with the holiness of God. Thus Paul writes to the "saints" of Ephesus, Corinth, Philippi, and Colossae. Today he would write to the "holy ones" of San Francisco, Iraq, or London—all gathered around the altar.

The church lived the communion of saints long before it started using the expression (around the fifth century). It was put into the Apostles' Creed as an emphatic statement that the church and the kingdom—or the People of God—is a community, not a loose gathering of people seeking private salvation. The phrase expresses the obvious: God sent Jesus to put his arms around all God's children, to draw them into one large family, and to teach them to pass the welcome along. Pope Leo XIII said, "The Communion of Saints is simply…the mutual sharing of help, atonement, prayers, and benefits among all the faithful."

## *To Continue your Journey of Exploration*

### The Church in the New Testament

How is church explained in the Scriptures? These New Testament passages shed some light on descriptions of the church in the Bible:

Colossians 1:18
1 Peter 2:9–10
Ephesians 2:19–20
1 Corinthians 3:9
1 Timothy 3:15
Galatians 3:28

### Images of the Church

Throughout the centuries—and today—various images have been used to describe the mystery that is the church. Here are a few of them:

*People of God:* The Church is a gathering of people who have been shaped by God and are bound together by faith.

The People of God is the predominant image of the church in the documents of the Second Vatican Council (1962-1965). This image is rooted in the Old Testament covenants in which God accompanies and loves the Israelites. The New Testament covenant invites all people everywhere to unite. God calls the church into existence, thereby forming a community of faith, hope, and love centered in Christ and empowered by the Holy Spirit.

*Body of Christ*: The Church is a body or group of people.

Christ is the head of the body. The members are many but are united in one church.

This image has been a prevalent one for the church, for it too has its foundations in Scripture. Together all form the body of Christ: if one suffers, all parts suffer. If one part is honored, all the parts share its joy (1 Corinthians 10:16–17; 1 Corinthians 12:12–13, 20).

John 15:5 proclaims: "I am the vine, you are the branches." All are called to work together for the common good.

*Pilgrim People:* We are all pilgrims journeying to our true home—eternal life with God.

This image of the church, the Pilgrim People of God, was highlighted in the Second Vatican Council's document *The Dogmatic Constitution on the Church.*

*Temple of the Holy Spirit:* God's Spirit makes the church a temple of holiness. The Spirit leads us in prayer and worship and helps us develop our special gifts.

St. Augustine said, "What the soul is to the human body, the Holy Spirit is to the church." Normally, the "temple of the Holy Spirit" is thought to refer to the individual believer rather than the church as a whole (see 1 Corinthians 6:19). However, believers are called a "spiritual house" and a "holy priesthood" by Peter in 1 Peter 2:4–8. Thus, in that sense, the People of God are being built into a "temple."

## Names for the Church

Paul uses the terms body of Christ and church interchangeably. The word church is a translation of the Greek word *ekklesia*, an assembly of people called forth, the People of God.

*The Mystical Body of Christ:* This is a concept developed by Saint Paul. Christ and his followers form one body: Christ is the head, we are the members (*Catechism of the Catholic Church*, nos. 787-789). An amazing conclusion follows from this idea of the church: Jesus needs us. We are the only way his hands can touch the sick or give bread to the starving. We are the only way people can see the forgiveness in his eyes. Our feet are the only way we can walk the road of modern civilization and proclaim the Good News.

*The Vine and the Branches:* This is Jesus' own comparison, spoken at the Last Supper (John 15).

*God's Family:* "You are fellow citizens with the holy ones and members of the household of God" (Ephesians 2:19).

*The People of God:* Vatican II chose to emphasize this title. God makes people holy and saves them "not merely as individuals without any mutual bonds but by making them into a single people, a people which acknowledges him in truth and serves him in holiness. He therefore chose the race of Israel as a people unto himself" (*Dogmatic Constitution on the Church,* no. 9).

The Council chose this title to emphasize the community aspect of the church. The church, says the *Dogmatic Constitution,* is a "fellowship of life, charity and truth" (no. 9). The term "people" reminds us that we do not "join" the church. Rather, we are called. The word *ecclesia* means "called out." The church is the called-together people, the assembly of God (*Catechism of the Catholic Church,* nos. 751-752).

## Vatican II and the Church

The Second Vatican Council declared that the church is a mystery (*Dogmatic Constitution on the Church*, chapter 1), which means that the church manifests God's love in ways we can never fully understand.

The Council also said that, in virtue of its relationship with Christ, the church is "a kind of sacrament or sign of intimate union with God, and of the unity of all (humankind)," as well as "an instrument for the achievement of such union and unity" (no. 1). The church is meant to be a sign that there can be unity among people, and the church is to work for that unity.

After the Council elaborated on the church as mystery and sacrament, it turned immediately to the words of St. Cyprian from the fifth century. Cyprian called "the church a people made one with the unity of the Father, the Son, and the Holy Spirit." Drawing heavily on biblical tradition, Vatican II devoted an entire chapter of its *Dogmatic Constitution on the Church* to a discussion of the church as "the new People of God" (chapter 2).

The Council declared that the church's laity and ordained clergy have much in common, thus breaking down artificial barriers. Although "they differ in essence and not simply in degree, (they) are nevertheless interrelated: each in its own particular way shares in the one priesthood of Christ" (*Dogmatic Constitution on the Church*, no. 10).

## The Church of Christ

One of the major topics at Vatican II was a discussion and renewed understanding of the church. In many ways, the Council called on us to understand the church in brand new ways, especially in the ways people related to one another in the church.

The core reality of who we are, of course, didn't change; the understanding of our relationships deepened.

The Council taught that the church is founded upon Christ and is made up of a number of "elements." Without these basic elements there would be no church.

First and foremost, the church is one, holy, catholic, and apostolic. There are other elements that are essential too. These include both visible and invisible elements.

The visible elements are those that make the church a recognizable body in the world. Among those the bishops mentioned are:

- Scripture, which is the church's written record of God's revelation

- Baptism, along with the other sacraments of the church

- The Episcopacy, which is the office of the bishop, and includes the pope, the bishop of Rome

- The Eucharist, the source and summit of the church's life

- The doctrines of the faith, the teachings that have come down to us from the time of the apostles

- Devotion to Mary, the Mother of God

The invisible elements cannot be seen except in their results. The members of the church show these elements by the way they live. Some of the elements mentioned by the Council fathers are:

- The life of grace, which is a participation in the very life of God

- The virtues of faith, hope, and love enabling us to act as children of God

- The gifts of the Holy Spirit

## The Marks of the Church

The four marks of the church is a term describing four specific adjectives (one, holy, catholic, and apostolic) indicating four distinctive characteristics of the church. The belief that the church is characterized by these four particular "marks" was first expressed by the First Council of Constantinople in the year 381 in its revision of the Nicene Creed, in which it included the statement: "[We believe] in one, holy, catholic, and apostolic Church."

*How is the church one? (Catechism of the Catholic Church,* nos. 813-818, 820, 866)
The church is one because its roots are in the Trinity. It is also one because it was founded by Christ and is animated by the Spirit.

Charity binds all together in the church as well as:

- our profession of faith, which is traceable to the apostles (the Apostles' and Nicene Creeds)

- common celebration in worship, especially the sacraments

- succession of the bishops from the apostles

Unity does not mean uniformity. God has gifted the church with a diversity of gifts and a variety of people.

### How is the church holy? (Catechism of the Catholic Church, nos. 823-829, 867)

Jesus Christ is the model of all holiness in the church. The Holy Spirit, dwelling in the church, fills it and unites it. God is the ultimate source of holiness in the church. Because the Spirit lives in us and in the church, the church is holy.

People are holy because of God's work in them. A major way God chooses to do this is through the church. Therefore, the church is holy because in it can be found the means to holiness, the means to the wholeness of personal development.

A major insight of Vatican II was that all of Jesus' disciples, not only the clergy and religious sisters and brothers, are called to holiness.

The true test of a Christian's holiness is a life of service to others.

### How is the church catholic? (Catechism of the Catholic Church, nos. 830-835, 868)

The church is catholic because Christ is present in the body as its head, giving it the fullness of the means of salvation: a complete and correct confession of faith, an ordained ministry traceable to the apostles, and a full sacramental life, especially the gift of the Eucharist.

The church is catholic because it follows the Lord's command to teach all nations. It reaches out to all people at all places in all times. Poor and rich, learned and unlearned, all people everywhere are invited to be members of the Lord's body.

The church is catholic because it continues to teach all that Christ taught.

*How is the church apostolic? (Catechism of the Catholic Church, nos. 857-865, 869)*

The present leadership of the Catholic Church can trace itself back to the first leaders of the church, the apostles. Christ founded his church on the apostles, who in turn appointed successors.

The church is also apostolic in that it professes the same doctrine and Christian way of life taught by the apostles. It has preserved the good news of Jesus and has not changed anything essential in his preaching.

Apostle means "one who is sent." All Christians are apostles and, by their baptism, have a role in sharing Christ's good news with others.

**What is the Church for?**

The church's purpose is to do in flesh and blood what Jesus did and does. Jesus is Priest; Jesus is Prophet; Jesus is King. (See *Catechism of the Catholic Church,* no. 436.)

So the church has the commission and the power to continue the priesthood of Jesus—in all its members, each according to his or her vocation.

The church has the commission and the power to continue the prophetic (speaking for God) work that Jesus did and does—again, in all its members: the hierarchy in its way, the laity in its way, all in Christ's way.

And the church has the commission and the power to continue the kingly rule of Christ—the most challenging of the three, because it includes washing others' feet as well as "binding and loosing."

The mission of the church is to participate in the saving, healing, and forgiving work of Jesus. We are the living presence of Christ reaching out in service to our sisters and brothers in the human family. Living church-for-the-world is our vocation.

## We are a Pilgrim Church...on the Journey

Some characteristics of being a pilgrim church:

- We have been on the journey for long time. We have a history, a story that connects us to many others before us.

- The journey is not always easy and glorious. Sometimes we have been considered a strange people.

- God's ways are not always our ways. God's idea of the kingdom has not always coincided with our human expectations of the kingdom (Luke 6:20).

- Many times our journeying together raises more questions than answers.

- Each church member's journey affects the journeys of others within the church.

## For Your Reflection and Conversation

- *When have you experienced the church to be the People of God?*

- *What's the mission of the church? What's the mission of your parish? What's your part in the mission?*

- *What important individuals (saints, heroes, and people of faith) have influenced your faith?*

- *How do you experience yourself as being an active part of the church as the People of God, instead of the church being "them" or the institution?*

- *What does it mean for you to be called to help the church be one, holy, catholic, and apostolic? Mention at least two specific implications for your life.*

- *What is the difference between becoming a member of the parish/the church and becoming a disciple of Jesus?*

- *What do you think the Spirit is saying to the church today?*

## As You Deepen your Prayer

Whenever we pray, we pray as part of the church and we pray for the church, even if we don't remember to do so explicitly. The church tells us that even the most isolated hermit prays as part of the whole body of Christ. Mindful of

that, choose one of the Scripture readings or prayers about
the church for your prayer and/or reflection:

- *"Go therefore and make disciples of all nations." (Matthew
  28:16–20)*

  - » When do you feel connected to the church uni-
    versal?
  - » What is one thing you could do to be more
    connected to someone (or others) in God's family
    beyond your immediate circle?

- *Paul wrote to the church in Rome: "Just as each of us has one body
  with many members, and these members do not all have the same
  function, so in Christ we who are many form one body, and each
  member belongs to all the others." (Romans 12:4–5)*

  - » Do you think of yourself belonging to all who are
    in God's church? When?
  - » What can you/do you give to others in God's family?
  - » How do you pray for others in God's family?

- *Prayer for Christian Unity:*
  Lord Jesus Christ, at your Last Supper
  you prayed to the Father that all should be one.
  Send your Holy Spirit upon all who bear your name
  and seek to serve you.
  Strengthen our faith in you
  and lead us to love one another in humility.
  May we who have been reborn in one baptism
  be united in one faith under one Shepherd. Amen.

# "...the forgiveness of sins, the resurrection of the body, and life everlasting. Amen."

## the forgiveness of sins...

A small boy had behaved badly much of the day and had been in all kinds of mischief. When his exasperated father put him to bed at night and told him to say his prayers, the boy replied: "Please go away, Dad. I want to talk to God alone."

"What have you done that you don't want me to know about?" the father asked.

"If I tell you," the boy said, "you'll get angry and shout and yell, but God will listen, forgive me, and forget about it."

As we come to the close of the Creed, we profess faith in a God of forgiveness, a truth the church has professed for centuries. In recent times, we have often heard it said that people don't believe in sin anymore. Perhaps that is true for a portion of our society, but committed Christians, true to their baptismal promises of following Jesus, do not live their lives in that way. In fact, the opposite is probably true today.

Those who not only believe facts about God but believe

in God and have experienced the God of love and forgiveness know themselves to be, in the words of the bumper sticker: "Christians are not perfect; they're just forgiven."

Having experienced God's unconditional love and forgiveness, Christians are empowered to continuing conversion and are committed to extending that love and forgiveness to all they meet and encounter in their daily lives.

## I believe in the resurrection of the body…

Ancient Greeks divided the world into the material and the spiritual. For people who thought this way, the declaration of the Apostles' Creed that "I believe in the resurrection of the body" was strange and perhaps even offensive. It was easy for someone from that culture to think that God had no plans for the body and to think that God was only concerned about the salvation of our spirits, not our bodies.

But 1 Thessalonians 5:23 says: "May the God of peace sanctify you completely, and may your whole spirit, soul, and body be preserved blameless…."

Likewise, in 2 Corinthians 4:13–14, Paul says: "We believe and so we speak, knowing that he who raised up the Lord Jesus will raise us up along with Jesus and place both us and you in his presence."

The dualistic thinking that has pervaded much of our history is not part of God's plan. We are not separate. The body matters to God. We are one, one whole spirit, body, and soul. The resurrection of Jesus is also about our resurrection. (See *Catechism of the Catholic Church*, nos. 988, 997-1004.)

The resurrection of the body will happen at the end of the world as we know it, a date unknown to us. How it will happen, of course, we do not know; but, like Jesus, our bodies will be glorified bodies, far different than the bodies we know now.

## I believe in life everlasting.

The afterlife is the ultimate life. It's the one for which we were created. That's why the church's message reminds us that death brings eternal joy: "Heaven is the ultimate end and fulfillment of the deepest human longings, the state of supreme and definitive happiness" (*Catechism of the Catholic Church*, no. 1024).

Scripture uses a variety of pictures to help us understand heaven, such as a wedding party, wine, life, light, peace, paradise, and the Father's house. But the real heaven is beyond any picture we can paint. We cannot imagine what the words mean, to be possessed eternally by fathomless happiness, nor to be filled with God's life, love, beauty, and goodness. We can only try to hold these ideas in inadequate little boxes of human words, boxes that often collapse (see *Catechism of the Catholic Church*, no. 1027).

Hell is the state of being turned away from God by one's own free and deliberate option—a life-option shaped by many decisions freely made (*Catechism of the Catholic Church*, no. 1033). Hell is eternal separation from God. It is impossible to be united with God if we refuse to love God.

Those who die in grace with God but who are not fully purified from their sinfulness are assured of their salvation. Their relationship with God must undergo a purification to obtain the love and holiness needed to enter heaven, where they have a heart that is totally open to God. This process is called purgatory (*Catechism of the Catholic Church*, no. 1030-31).

**Amen.**

We conclude by praying "yes" or "so be it."

We say yes to the Creator, Son, and Holy Spirit; yes to the goodness of life in the church today; yes to the promise of eternal life in the world to come

## To Continue your Journey of Exploration

### What Scripture tells us about Jesus' Forgiveness

Mark 2:1–12: Jesus heals a paralytic

- Why didn't Jesus just heal the paralytic like everyone expected him to?

- What new insight about himself and the kingdom is he revealing?

- In what ways is sin like paralysis?

  Luke 7:36–50: Jesus anointed by a sinful woman

- Why did Jesus tell the parable to Simon rather than just accusing him of not loving enough?

- What does Jesus see in the woman that others do not?

- Has someone in your life believed in you even before you did? How did that affect you?

Luke 19:1–10: Zacchaeus the tax collector

- Why did Jesus dine with Zacchaeus?

- On what basis does Jesus confirm Zacchaeus' salvation?

- Why is restitution an important part of conversion?

John 8:1–11: Woman caught in adultery

- Why was this situation a trap for Jesus?

- What is the difference between God's forgiveness and society's forgiveness? (What does God require versus what does society require?)

What does Jesus' ministry, as illustrated in these four stories, tell us about God's mercy and forgiveness?

## Heaven, Hell, and Purgatory

In July 1999, Pope John Paul II gave a series of Angelus talks in which he talked about heaven and hell. Some of the things he said are:

Heaven "is not an abstraction, not a physical place amid the clouds, but a living and personal relationship with the Holy Trinity."

"Eternal damnation…is not attributed to God's initiative because in his merciful love he can only desire the salvation of the beings he created. In reality, it is the creature who closes himself to his love. Damnation consists precisely in definitive separation from God, freely chosen by the human person and confirmed with death that seals his choice for ever."

"Eternal damnation remains a real possibility, but we are not granted, without special divine revelation, the knowledge of whether or which human beings are effectively involved in it."

## A Look at Purgatory

"The church gives the name Purgatory to this final purification of the elect, which is entirely different from the punishment of the damned" (*Catechism of the Catholic Church*, no. 1031).

In the church's belief about Purgatory, there is nothing about fire or length of time or agony. It is the belief that if there is any sinfulness in me, it must be removed before I come face-to-face with God.

Because of our belief of the interdependence of God's creation and the wonderful mystery of the communion of saints, the church teaches that the prayers of the living can help those who have died.

## Two Parables about Heaven and Hell

*The Difference between Heaven and Hell: The Samurai and the Monk*

The story is told of a big, tough samurai who once went to see a little monk. "Monk," he said, in a voice accustomed to instant obedience, "teach me about heaven and hell."

The monk looked up at this mighty warrior and replied with utter disdain, "Teach you about heaven and hell? I couldn't teach you about anything. You're dirty. You smell. Your blade is rusty. You are a disgrace, an embarrassment to the samurai class. Get out of my sight. I can't stand you."

The samurai was furious. He shook, got all red in the face, and was speechless with rage. He pulled out his sword and raised it above him, preparing to slay the monk.

"That's hell," said the monk softly.

The samurai was overwhelmed.

The compassion and surrender of this little monk who had offered his life to show him hell! He slowly put down his sword, became filled with gratitude, and was suddenly peaceful.

"And that's heaven," said the monk softly.

Theologians often suggest that heaven and hell are states of being that are the flowering of sin and grace. Hell and heaven are happening in the present. Hell is found in human rage and the desire to kill. Heaven is found in the feeling of gratitude and peace that comes when you realize that someone cared enough to risk their life for you.

### A Visit to Heaven and Hell

One day a saint was visited by an angel who asked her if she wished to see heaven and hell. She said, "Yes," and was immediately transported to hell. It was not at all what she had expected.

It was a beautiful place with many mansions. But then she heard terrible sounds of agony and pain. She followed her ears and found herself in a huge banquet hall. The tables were filled with delicious food, and all the residents of hell were seated at the tables.

They all looked normal except for one very important difference. They had long arms, maybe five feet in length. At the end of each arm, in their hands, were forks. But they could not get the food to their mouths because no one had an elbow. They howled with hunger before a banquet of food.

Next, she was transported to heaven. It was not what she expected.

It was a beautiful place of many mansions—exactly like hell. But soon she heard sounds of rejoicing. She followed her ears and came to a huge banquet hall. The tables were filled with delicious food, and all the residents of heaven were seated at the tables.

The people were shaped exactly like the residents of hell—long arms and no elbows—but this caused them no difficulty. They simply loaded their forks with food and reached across the table to feed a friend. Everyone was fed.

## Thoughts to Ponder

God does not force either salvation or damnation; it is our own doing. Heaven and hell are our responses to God's eternal love. C.S. Lewis cleverly stated this theological insight: "There are only two kinds of people in the end: those who say to God, 'Thy will be done,' and those to whom God says, in the end, 'Thy will be done.'"

How differently we view death if we see every human life as precisely the same length—eternal. Make a conscious effort to remember that, for those who follow Jesus, death is never the last word. *Life* always is.

## Ending with "Amen"

"Amen" is a resounding "yes," an affirmation that punctuates our prayers and celebrations. It means: "so be it," "I agree," "it is firm."

In Hebrew, "amen" comes from the same root as the word

for "believe." Thus, when we say "amen," we are making an act of faith, proclaiming the truth of what we have prayed and celebrated. It is a summary of our heartfelt conviction and expresses our solidarity with it. Saying "amen" to the Apostles' Creed (and the Nicene Creed) restates our belief in God and all the other articles of the Creed.

Death is a kind of "amen" to human life. For Christians who have "fought the good fight," death is a statement that readies us for eternity. If we are living lives of love and discipleship, then death is not something to fear. Rather, it punctuates the sentence of our lives. It enables us to present ourselves to God as the finished story of a loving follower of Jesus.

## FOR YOUR REFLECTION AND CONVERSATION

- *Have you ever forgiven someone who never found out about it?*

- *Is there someone in your life who hurt you, and you have never forgiven them?*

- *Do you think human beings cannot completely forgive and forget?*

- *Have you ever asked someone to forgive you?*

- *Have you ever been forgiven and felt a sense of relief?*

- *Ivern Ball said: "Most of us can forgive and forget; we just don't want the other person to forget that we forgave." What does that call us to?*

• *Do you think forgiveness sometimes involves a promise in return?*

• *David Ridge said: "True forgiveness is not an action after the fact; it is an attitude with which you enter each moment." If people lived this way, how might the world and our relationships be different?*

• *Do you think there is something for which you could never forgive a person?*

• *George Herbert said: "When we can't forgive, we will break the bridge over which we must pass." What do you think?*

• *In South Africa, a woman's son was shot and killed. They dragged his lifeless body back to his home and then brought out his father and killed him as well. Then they took the bodies and buried them in a place only known to them. The wife and mother left behind didn't even know where they were buried. Eventually, the authorities brought one of the murderers to justice. They asked the woman what she wanted to be done to him. She replied softly, "This man took everything away from me except my ability to love." She asked that he bring her two handfuls of dirt from her husband and son's grave and then she asked that he come and see her once a month. That's it.* What would you have done?

• *As you think about the resurrection of the body, do you think that in heaven we will be nothing like we were on earth or will there be similarities, a continuation of our life of earth?*

• *What do you think a glorified body is like?*

• *As you think about everlasting life, heaven and hell, what comforts you? What do you wonder about?*

• *What image or metaphor would you use for heaven?*

• *Have you journeyed with a dying person? What was their experience?*

• *Does praying "amen" challenge you? How?*

• *In two sentences, what do you say "amen" to by your life?*

• *What do you think God hears when we pray "amen"?*

## As You Deepen your Prayer

### A Prayer of Amen
The following prayer is sung by Catholics as they process from the church at the conclusion of the celebration of the funeral liturgy:

May the angels lead you into paradise;
may the martyrs come to welcome you
and take you to the holy city,

the new and eternal Jerusalem.

How do the words express our belief that for those who have served Christ, death is the end of our earthly pilgrimage and the beginning of eternal happiness and peace?

## Concluding Thought…
## As We Pray and Live the Creed

Sometimes we think of the Creed as a list of things we believe in. Yet, to begin at the end for a moment, we recall that we conclude the Creed with "amen." "Amen" reminds us that we are praying. As individuals, and as a community, we are in dialogue with God. And because our creeds originated in the early church within the baptismal rite, they are fundamental prayers, affirming who we are, whose we are, and all we're called to be. In declaring our faith-filled pledge in the Creed, we wholeheartedly pray and fervently commit to live what we pray.